Teaching in multiracial schools

a guidebook

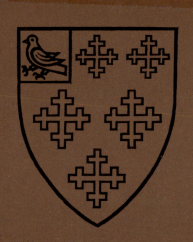

CHRIST CHURCH
COLLEGE
CANTERBURY

AUTHOR. **HILL, D.**

TITLE. **Teaching in multiracial schools**

CLASS NO. **371.97** COPY

DAVID HILL

Teaching

in

multiracial

schools

a guidebook

METHUEN

First published in 1976 by Methuen & Co Ltd
11, New Fetter Lane, London EC4P 4EE
© 1976 David Hill
Printed in Great Britain by
Butler & Tanner Ltd, Frome and London

ISBN 0 416 82090 5 (*hardback edition*)
ISBN 0 416 82100 6 (*paperback edition*)

Distributed in the USA *by*
HARPER & ROW PUBLISHERS INC
BARNES & NOBLE IMPORT DIVISION

Contents

Acknowledgements

The publishers and the author would like to thank the following for permission to reproduce copyright material in this book:

Christian Education Movement for passages taken from *World Religions in the Primary School* by Owen Cole, and *World Religions in the Secondary School* by Donald Butler; National Foundation for Educational Research and the authors for passages from *Organization in Multiracial Schools* by H. E. R. Townsend and E. Brittan; the editor of *Housecraft* and Yvonne Collymore for extracts from *Housecraft* (January 1974); Blackie & Son for the illustration from *Teacher's Guide to SPARKS* by Fisher, Hynds, Johns and McKenzie; the Longman Group for illustrations from the scope project; E. J. Arnold for the illustrations from CONCEPT 7–9; ATEPO for the map taken from *Report of the Work Group of West Indian Pupils*; George Allen & Unwin and the author for the maps adapted from *The Background of Immigrant Children* by I. Morrish.

I

Introduction

It is evident, especially in our large cities and industrial areas, that we have already become a multiracial society. Although there have been pockets of coloured populations at some sea ports for a long time, the influx of a large number of immigrants from the ex-colonial countries is a recent phenomenon. The second world war could be regarded as the turning point in the history of Commonwealth immigration to Britain. The arrival of a large number of Commonwealth troops who saw much wider economic and educational opportunities here, the closing of the United States of America for the West Indian immigrants by the Johnson Act, the mushrooming of the number of overseas students who carried first hand information back to their countries, the relative ease of travel, all contributed towards a rapid increase in immigration to Britain.

The educational issues which have arisen, and their solution, cannot be isolated from larger social issues. As Goldman and Taylor[2] say: 'The plight of coloured children is essentially the plight of the socially disadvantaged children in slum and problem areas, but with the added dimensions of language difficulties and colour prejudice to overcome. The problems are bound up with housing, health, youth employment and many other factors.'

The rate of immigration into Great Britain has been the subject of wide speculation but it was estimated (Hansard, 22nd June, 1967) that the number of residents in Great Britain who were coloured immigrants from the New Commonwealth, or one or both of whose parents had emigrated from the Commonwealth, was probably of the order of one million at the end of 1966 out of a total population of fifty-two and a half million; i.e. less than 2 per cent. By 1985 it is estimated that there will be 3,500,000 West Indians, Africans and Asians in a total British population of 70 million.

In 1971 the total number of immigrant* pupils in maintained primary and secondary schools with 10 or more such pupils in England and Wales was 263,710. This was about 3.3 per cent of all school children, compared to 3.2 per cent in 1970. The total number of immigrant children, in *all* maintained schools in 1972 was 279,872, 3.3 per cent of all pupils; this figure includes pupils from Europe, North America and Australasia. The number of immigrant children in these schools in January 1972 was as indicated in Table 1.

Since the majority of coloured immigrants are either semi-skilled or unskilled, often accustomed to a low standard of living, they tend to settle in the poorer districts of our cities in property they can afford. In fact 80 per cent of such immigrants were, according to Peach[2] concentrated in urban areas, with half in Britain's ten largest cities. This position is relatively unchanged. This means that in some cities and towns the concentration of coloured immigrants is as much as 8 per cent, and in particular neighbourhoods as high as 50 per cent. Schools in these areas are frequently short staffed, overcrowded, and have inadequate buildings and facilities. Despite recent Urban Aid programmes any population influx into these areas accentuates these difficulties, and because the coloured immigrant is

* See page 6 for definition.

Table 1   *Immigrant pupils by origin in all maintained schools, January 1972, and percentage of total immigrants*

Country	Numbers	%
Australia, Canada & New Zealand	2,455	0.9
Cyprus (Greek)	9,504	3.4
(Turkish)	4,461	1.6
Gibraltar, Malta	1,252	0.4
Kenya (Asian origin)	17,340	6.2
(African origin)	1,385	0.5
Other Commonwealth countries in Africa	14,444	5.3
India	56,193	20.1
Pakistan	30,629	10.9
Other Commonwealth countries in Asia	8,008	2.9
West Indies (including Guyana)	101,898	36.4
Non-Commonwealth countries		
Italy	12,009	4.3
Poland	1,958	0.7
Spain	3,275	1.2
Other European countries	5,980	2.1
Rest of World	9,081	3.2
Total	279,872	100.0

Source: *Statistics of Education 1972*, Vol. I, *Schools* (London: HMSO).

easily identifiable he is accused by many of the host population as the cause of these problems. However, the NFER survey of LEAs in 1971[3] indicated that immigrants (coloured and others) are moving out of the urban areas, this occurrence being reflected in the fact that at the time there were 70 LEAs with more than 500 immigrant children in their schools.

Perhaps the basic aim of schools in Britain for incoming ethnic groups should be to enable them to 'integrate', i.e. enable them to adapt effectively to living in our society in certain ways (e.g. education and employment), while encouraging them, and others, to accept differences in religion, culture and family patterns. A first consideration in fulfilling this aim will obviously be the teaching of the English language, since without mastery of this immigrant pupils will not be able to derive benefit from much else that their school may have to offer. Schools would also need to provide an effective introduction to our way of life (remembering that any introduction that is effective is likely to take account of their own background and culture).

The alternative to educating for integration is educating for 'assimilation', which would involve complete acceptance of our values and patterns of living on the part of minority ethnic groups. I think this would be an inappropriate and unrealistic aim for schools because assimilation assumes complete acceptance of the minority group by the host society. In the case of minority groups whose colour is different to ours, this acceptance is difficult to achieve. It would be unfair if schools did not acknowledge this fact.

During the past few years there has been considerable publicity given to the large percentage of coloured immigrant children in schools. In Birmingham, for example, one infant school has a 90 per cent immigrant intake, and the local authority has estimated that although the *average* proportion of immigrant to all children in Birmingham maintained schools is only 5 per cent, there are twenty-four primary schools with between 16 and 70 per cent coloured immigrant children. In West Bromwich the Education Committee estimated, far back in 1966, that by the mid-seventies 16 per cent of all primary and 20 per cent of all secondary pupils were likely to be coloured.

Thus in some areas, despite Immigration Acts, the number of immigrant children in schools has risen and will continue to rise. Such considerations as these can cause racial tension since English parents are often afraid that their children will be held back at school because of immigrant children whose standards of literacy and intelligence are assumed to be lower. It is undeniable that many immigrant children will, naturally, be less literate than many indigenous pupils and will indeed be in need of specialized teaching. It is therefore most important that adequate planning should be made to cope with this situation. What has and is being done to prepare teachers and schools to operate effectively in a multiracial society?

Ministry of Education pamphlets offering general advice and guidelines have been circulated in the past; and local authorities have adopted policies which suit their particular circumstances. Some local authorities have recognized the potential benefit of employing overseas teachers in schools which have an intake of immigrant pupils. However it has been found that some training is necessary to equip such teachers for teaching in English schools. Relevant courses have been set up in some colleges of education and university departments. The decision to employ overseas teachers has not been without controversy; it is claimed in some quarters that such teachers often find it difficult to make themselves understood in the average classroom and, further, that they do not provide a helpful model for minority ethnic group children as far as speech rhythms are concerned.

Over the last decade much research and many papers have been generated by the influx of New Commonwealth immigrants. For those who would like to have more details of this, the NFER has published a summary of research and literature in the field of multi-cultural education and the education of children from minority groups.[4]

Yet while sociologists and educators have become increasingly aware of the nature of the situation and its demands, official action has tended to lag behind. The failure of the Department of Education and Science to fully appreciate the difficulties of schools with large numbers of minority ethnic group pupils is illustrated by the definition of 'immigrant' the

Department used right up to 1974 as a basis for school returns (Form 7, i). This has been:

- (i) Children born outside the British Isles who have come to this country with or to join parents or guardians whose countries of origin were abroad.
- (ii) Children born in the UK to parents whose countries of origin were abroad and who came to the UK up to ten years before the date to which the figures apply.
- NB Children of mixed immigrant and non-immigrant parentage and children from the Republic of Ireland are excluded.

   Children of immigrant parents from two overseas countries have been classified according to the country of origin of the father.

   (DES, *Department of Education and Science Statistics 1971*, Vol. I, HMSO, 1972)

This definition gave a distorted picture of the situation in schools because it did not include children of minority ethnic groups whose families have been resident here for some time, but who are nonetheless suffering from the same disadvantages as those experienced by the children who fall within the definition. There is an apparently contradictory phrase, 'immigrant born here', which does in fact express an educational reality, as many teachers are aware. Such children are likely to be as much in need of special language tuition, for example, as those who have come to this country more recently.*

Based upon the limited 'official' definition of immigrant, misguided tables have been compiled in the past by LEAs and others, showing the supposed decline of the number of immigrant children in schools. In as much as this apparent trend has

---

* My use of the word 'immigrant' in this book does not therefore follow the DES definition, but is intended to include the wider group described above. I have sometimes, used the rather unwieldy but descriptively correct term 'minority ethnic group'.

been an excuse for delaying urgently needed action, the authorities can be accused of working against the interests of immigrant children and the schools in which they are taught. It has
not been helpful from an educational point of view that many
well-intentioned organizations, working towards the ideal of a
harmonious multiracial society, have not recognized the anom-
alies of the situation and have also accepted the picture given by
the information provided on Form 7 (i).

The result of all this is that many children's education has
suffered because of the lack of materials and staff, both of which
may well have been supplied if the position had been more fully
appreciated nationally prior to the report on education by the
Parliamentary Select Committee on Race Relations and Immigration in 1973 (*Report of the Select Committee on Race Relations
and Immigration. Session 1972–3, Education.* Vol. I, HMSO).

One of the most glaring examples of educational neglect has
been the plight of West Indian pupils, who were not until
comparatively recently singled out as requiring specialized
tuition in the English language. (c.f. Schools Council Project
for *Teaching English to West Indian Children*, Working Paper 29,
Evans/Methuen Educational, 1970). The belated recognition of
the linguistic handicaps faced by West Indian children (who
may, in addition, have problems of adjustment to conflicting
home, school and peer group expectations) has possibly contributed to incorrect assessment of their academic potential and
a disproportionate percentage being assigned to ESN schools.
In this connexion, we now have evidence that the steadily
increasing number of Chinese children in Britain are in a similar
plight, and a plea has been made that their position warrants
special attention.[5]

I think it is important that we should be aware of the fact that
most of our thinking concerning the difficulties and challenges
of the multiracial school has more often than not been retro-
spective, and invariably determined by political, not educational, motives. Thus, as I have said above, many pupils – both

indigenous and those belonging to minority ethnic groups – have been receiving an inadequate education partly through the fault of misguided, often determinedly liberal, policies.

Despite the general interest in the issue of education for a multiracial society, there has been a notable lack of practical books on the subject which suggest to teachers what they need to know and what resources are available to them which would enable them to be more effective teachers in the multiracial classroom. This book has been written in the hope that it will supply this need, in part at any rate. I recognize that no one book can offer adequate information on all pertinent issues, and I have therefore selected those topics which practising teachers have suggested would be useful.

This first chapter has briefly introduced certain key issues which will be developed in later chapters. The second section describes the three largest minority ethnic groups in Britain (West Indian, Indian and Pakistani/Bangladeshi). Special reference is made to cultural traditions, religion and life styles, i.e. those factors which particularly distinguish the minority groups from indigenous pupils and which could affect their learning in British schools. Other groups (e.g. Chinese, Cypriot, Italian) could have been included, but I decided to restrict this section to groups most often encountered by teachers – which are also groups which seem to experience serious educational difficulties. It is possible, of course, that some of what I have written may apply more widely.

For a number of years now there has been widespread concern over the methods of assessing the abilities and attainments of immigrant pupils, and the third chapter summarizes the position and indicates future possibilities in this field.

Chapter 4 was to have been a brief bibliographical guide to methods and material used by teachers in dealing with language difficulties in the multiracial school. However, since this is primarily a teacher's book I decided to reject this brief guide in favour of a more general overview, with detailed descriptions of a number of selected language schemes. At the end of this section is a brief section on language difficulties of Chinese children. In view of the increasing number of Chinese pupils in our schools, this may be found useful.

The fifth chapter is of more general interest since it considers other aspects of the teacher's task, e.g. school meals, religious teaching, dress, and so on. These areas, though not necessarily problematic, have been known to present teachers with a certain amount of difficulty.

Finally the sixth chapter summarizes the issues that have been discussed in connexion with teaching in multiracial schools, and indicates some of the ways in which education for a multiracial society might be improved. This ends with a section listing journals, indexes of audio-visual aids, and useful addresses.

References

1 GOLDMAN, R. and TAYLOR, F. (1966) Coloured immigrant children: A survey of research studies and literature on their educational problems and potential in Britain. *Educational Research* VIII, 3.

2 PEACH, C. (1965) Immigrants and the 1961 Census. *Newsletter*, Institute of Race Relations.

3 TOWNSEND, H. (1971) *Immigrant Pupils in England: The LEA Response*. Slough: NFER.

4 TAYLOR, F. (1974) *Race, School and Community: A Study of Research and Literature on Education in Multiracial Britain*. Slough: NFER.

5 GARVEY, S. and JACKSON, B. (1974) *Chinese Children*. Cambridge Educational Development Trust.

2

A brief description of the three largest minority ethnic groups in Britain

The West Indian

The islands which we refer to as the West Indies are those of the Antillean archipelago and, together with British Honduras in North America and Guyana in South America, constitute the British Caribbean.

Such a collection of separate societies will inevitably show wide variations in geography, customs, and social organization, but there are still sufficient common cultural elements to allow a generalized description of the whole group.

The West Indian economy is largely dependent on agriculture, and although industrialization has begun in Jamaica and Trinidad, their urban/rural population ratios are relatively small. Despite (or because of) their long history of capital investment from outside sources, they remain essentially poor, undeveloped and overpopulated countries. They are multiracial societies whose members are descended from ancestors imported from Africa as slaves, and exploited by competing European colonists keen to develop the economic potential of the area. Persons born within the West Indies are referred to as 'Creoles', but this term

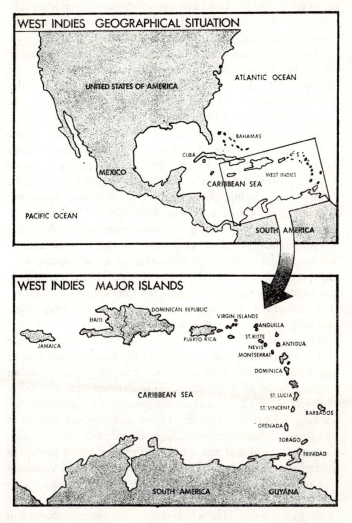

Fig. 2.1 *From ATEPO (Birmingham branch) work group on West Indian pupils*, Report 1970.

is not applied to the East Indian population, which is a sizeable minority, who are called 'East Indians'. Other minorities, however, e.g. the Chinese, have managed to preserve their own cultural identity and are referred to in the appropriate national terms. The Creoles therefore are persons of Negro, White, or Negro/White ancestry born within the Caribbean. All the British Caribbean has a similar form of Creole culture, in contrast to that of the Dutch and French West Indian Creoles. However all of these cultures, are products of colonialism, slavery, and the plantation system, and therefore contain both European and African elements. In this connexion one writer says; '. . . forms of institutional life such as government, religion, family and kinship, law, property, education, economy, language etc., are of European derivation.[1] These forms of institutional life have naturally undergone considerable local adaptation and therefore only approximate to their metropolitan models. This adaptation involved an interaction with that part of the African culture that the immigrants maintained, the process taking place within the limits defined by slavery. The 'African' residue in e.g. language, diet, folklore, magic and religion has been described in detail elsewhere.[2]

The combination of a strong adherence to European culture and a white ruling class ensured that the European element of the Creole culture became the most highly valued, and an explicit index of high status. This development entailed a devaluation of all the African components of the culture, including racial traits, so that the high- and low-status sections of the society were distinguishable both culturally and racially. 'The Creole cultural and social organization was a graduated hierarchy of European and African elements, crudely visualized in a white–black colour scale'.[3] Clearly these factors are crucial to the aetiology of the 'white bias' which characterizes the society even today. 'The whole colour class system is dependent upon the almost complete acceptance by each group of the superiority of the white, and the inferiority of the black'.[3] This cultural and racial bias, taken together with the strong historical connexion between the West Indies and Britain, accounts to a considerable extent for the immigrant's orientation towards British society and his aspiration to be part of it.

Racial organization of the society permeates all aspects of its life. The attribute of lighter skin-colour is a social advantage in most situations and status differentials can often depend on subtle gradations of colour. It is the ambition of many darker-skinned West Indians to 'marry lighter' and thereby 'improve' the colour (and therefore the opportunities for advancement) of their offspring. The coincidence of colour and class is perhaps nowhere better illustrated than in the example cited by Rose *et al.*[4] 'Colour in the sense of appearance as a key to descent has been of such importance in this society that colour terms are often used to indicate class and a man is spoken of as "white" because he is rich or successful'. Nettlefold[5] substantiates this analysis in his account of national identity and race attitude in Jamaica; as does Bentley.[6]

The English 'model' and ways can still today play an important part in West Indian psychology, and this can even lead to a rejection of all that is West Indian. Such rejection has also been enhanced, in the past, by the use in West Indian schools of materials which emphasize the 'white' image: portraying white heroes, white angels, a white god, and generally glorifying a light-coloured skin. Conversely, as previously mentioned, a dark skin is deemed to be of inferior status. Such self-rejection can obviously produce feelings of inferiority, which in turn can affect attitudes and behaviour. It would therefore seem of paramount importance that British teachers should propagate a philosophy which is multiracial in character and stresses the equality of races.

The family is the focal point of activities in the West Indian poorer class, and, in the absence of an advanced welfare state system, the family has retained many of the responsibilities which are more often assumed by the state in this country.

But at this stage it is important to add that the 'family' in the West Indies is not necessarily the small, closely related group that we tend to regard as the typical family in this country (i.e. father, mother and children); but might well consist of a woman and her man, their children, her mother, her brother and a sister (unmarried) with a child.

This family's income might be derived from a variety of sources, including the mother's brother's earnings and the occasional sum of money paid to her sister by the father of her (sister's) child. This is obviously a broader and more complex concept of the family than our own, and in trying to describe the West Indian situation some writers have made a distinction between the 'biological' and the 'functioning' family. *Biologically*, then, the father of the sister's child in this hypothetical household group is a member of the family; but he plays no well-defined *function* in it (his occasional gifts of money are being made in a spirit of generosity and concern rather than because of any legal or moral obligation on him to send them). It will be obvious from the foregoing that the accepted pattern of sexual and marital relationships differs considerably from our own present outlook; the reason for this can be found in the behaviour of the former white, slave-owning élite of the West Indies. Slaves were encouraged to breed (to produce more labourers) though they were prohibited from marrying each other. Slave fathers obviously had no legal rights over their children; it was the slave owner who possessed the child, gave it a name, a home and an education – if any. Often the father of the child and the owner of its mother were the same man. In these circumstances it is not hard to see that the conjugal and marital role among slaves had to be adapted. West Indian family life still retains certain features of their ancestors' life in slavery, and the high number of illegitimate births is evidence of the inheritance.

After Emancipation in 1834 many ex-slaves adopted facets of European life – one of these being Christian marriage. They naturally insisted upon their own interpretation of it, based on their past experience. Consequently marriage became an institution more indicative of social standing and financial security than of a shared home. In this context sexual relationships outside marriage, and the resultant illegitimate children, have become accepted as a natural way of life among those who do not have much social standing or financial security. In fact, very few Christian sects in the West Indies place pressure upon their congregation to enter into a legal marriage with their chosen partners. 'Faithful concubinage', then, could be described as the poor man's substitute for marriage. The partners of such a liaison could well get married, usually late in life, but equally they may separate at quite an early stage when the children are still young. What happens next is not governed by any clear convention; they may enter new relationships or perhaps return to their respective mothers' households. There is no convention, either, regarding their responsibilities towards their children.

In addition to stable concubinage there are other kinds of relatively permanent relationships which often produce children. However, if such parents separate, the children usually stay with the mother. The father's role in such an intricate family system is a difficult one to define: in a married home he would be expected to be authoritative and responsible for the family's welfare; in a 'faithful concubinage' situation he would share equal responsibility with his partner for the children. But in addition to these two interpretations of the father's role there are other acceptable kinds of paternal behaviour, including a completely non-participatory role. In such a situation one can often find a man accepting responsibility for someone else's children (i.e. the children of a woman he marries) while not regarding himself as responsible for his own (the result of a former liaison). Not surprisingly, therefore, the mother's role in the family is a stronger one in that it is more definite. The system is matri-central rather than matriarchal.

When there is no functioning father in a West Indian family

the link between mothers and daughters is strong, and the mother–son relationship can also become very important, as sons in many ways take the role of husband-substitute. A mother's influence over her son can often rival that of his wife or girl-friend.

It is not usual for most West Indian children to spend all their childhood in the same house with both parents. They often move from one parent to a grandmother *etc.*, which would be regarded as rather an odd arrangement in Britain. However, set in the context of family life in the West Indies this sort of separation does not have the traumatic effects that might be expected from it in this country. Though the relationship between parents and children may not be as close-knit as we would expect, yet there are perhaps strong links with other members of the family, and these are much more important than they would be in this country.

Another important social unit in the West Indies is the 'yard', which is a group of houses clustered around an open space where the occupants share the basic facilities. Such a community is primarily founded on kinship and common interest, which invariably means that the adults share the responsibility for all the children. As already indicated a family separation in this type of community does not produce the traumatic experiences which might well result from such a break-up in England.

Some research on child rearing practices in the West Indies seems to suggest that a major aim is to prevent children from being 'rude'. The latter word seems to be used to include all kinds of misdeeds. 'Good' children are frequently conceived of as being passive. The well worn saying 'seen and not heard' would be a very appropriate description of this 'good' behaviour. The way in which such model behaviour is often achieved is interesting, since the methods are invariably inconsistent. For example it has been said[10] that children are treated permissively in such things as feeding and toilet training, but experience considerable repression for rudeness – usually accompanied by unfulfilled threats. As a general example of the differences between the English and West Indian attitude to the child's role in the family one could say that the English parents consider they have an obligation to their children, accepting blame for their social inadequacies, whereas West Indian parents believe that the children must please them and should feel guilty if they fail to achieve parental expectations. Herein lies the root cause of many arguments between West Indian parents and their children: when the West Indian parents expect apologies from their children, the latter, who have been influenced by education and English life styles, expect much more understanding from their parents.

Altogether there are many changes in family life styles when the West Indian comes to Britain. Firstly most of the immigrants are young adults, and, accordingly, the three-generation family is not so common in England. Also the West Indian regards coming to England as a move up the social scale and consequently marriage becomes appropriate for a couple who previously were perfectly happy to live together. Naturally this kind of regrouping can create considerable difficulties for those members of the family unit who regard a tight nuclear group as inappropriate to their position. An example of such a regrouping may be seen in the case of an illigitimate child born in the West Indies to young parents who have since separated. One of the parents may emigrate to Britain with every intention of sending for the child when he/she has settled down and is economically secure. However, frequently such a parent meets a new partner, marries and has more children. Subsequently the first child may be brought to England but obviously has to make considerable adjustments to the host country, school and, of course, his new family. It has been suggested that some of the behavioural problems encountered in West Indian adolescents could result from this particular aspect of immigration.

The West Indians constitute the largest minority ethnic group in the United Kingdom. Most of them are unskilled or semi-skilled workers in the transport industry and building trades. Relatively few West Indian men are skilled workers. Apart from working in factories, a large number of West Indian women are employed in hospitals and the catering trade. By virtue of the nature of their employment, West Indians, like other ethnic minorities, are concentrated almost exclusively in urban areas.

One might expect that the West Indians, since they share our language, faith and culture, will face fewer difficult problems in coming to terms with British society than some other minority ethnic groups. However, of the three major minority ethnic groups in Britain, i.e. Indian, Pakistani and West Indian, it is the latter who seem to experience most difficulties in school. Linguistically they seem to have an advantage over the other two groups, but the difference between their home dialect and their school dialect can create educational difficulties (see Schools Council Working Paper 29, 'Teaching English to West Indian Children, Evans/Methuen Educational, 1970).

The West Indian also poses a challenge to our understanding and that of our social workers because of the high incidence of broken families and children of varied parentage. Certainly we need to find out more about the varied family structure of West Indians, and other minority ethnic groups, since it is evident that climates within the family affect attitudes to education.

I think there is some evidence[7] that West Indian family relationships are much more stabilized than hitherto. This may well be because during the past few years there has been an increasing tendency for the West Indian immigrants to arrive in this country as family units, for example, father and son (leaving mother and the remaining children to follow later), which was certainly not in evidence in earlier migration patterns.

Additional evidence in support of this stabilization in West Indian family life is supplied by Bhatnagar.[8] His research study in 1970 found that 86 per cent of West Indians were living with both parents compared with 93.5 per cent in a sample of English boys and girls at the same school. So, although in general, there are twice as many West Indians as English pupils not living with both parents the figure in Bhatnagar's sample (86 per cent) is higher than one might have expected. Bhatnagar also quotes a random sample, taken in the West Indies, of Jamaicans intending to migrate to the United Kingdom in 1961. Of these 22 per cent were legally married. Later in England 272 persons from this sample, three-quarters of the original number, were again contacted and at the end of their first year's stay, 45 per cent were legally married, 52 per cent at the end of the second year. The census returns for 1961 and the sample census for 1966 detailed in the Institute of Race Relations Report on *Colour and Citizenship* show that in 1961, 58.8 per cent of West Indian women over fifteen years of age (and resident in six major conurbations in Britain) were legally married; 65.7 in 1966. It is thus reasonably safe to assume that, of migrant parents who have been living in Britain for a number of years, at least two-thirds will be legally married, and quite possibly more, since 'women over fifteen' obviously includes an unknown proportion of women who are not parents. Whether acceptance of a more English pattern of marriage also involves an 'English' acceptance of divorce remains to be seen. The above information is included in this section since it indicates the increasing frequency of stable family relationships among West Indians in Britain, with Bhatnagar's finding of 86 per cent referred to earlier, illustrating the continuance of this trend.

It should also be noted that in 1969 a study[9] of West Indian mothers found that 90 per cent were married and that three-quarters of those who were unmarried when they came to Britain had got married within two years of their arrival. For most of these women illegitimacy carried no stigma at home, yet in England half of them felt it was important to legitimize their children. This study also found that over half the women were working* and that the husbands were actively helping in the children's upbringing. This pattern is very different from that in the West Indies, although it must be remembered that many Caribbean families in Britain are still matri-central in form. Nonetheless with job security providing the economic basis which was hitherto seen as the prerequisite of marriage in the West Indies, West Indians in Britain are increasingly following a family pattern which is typical of present British customs.

Recent evidence[7] has shown that to some extent the integration of minority ethnic groups into the host society has already occurred. Attitudes, particularly those involving aspirations and expectations, are clearly affected by length of stay, those immigrants who have been in Britain longest generally recording the more favourable attitudes. Such a finding may reflect credit upon the government's outlook over the past decade in encouraging the development of a multiracial society. It may also be the result in part of a change in attitude on the part of leading immigrant organizations. Where, previously, the emphasis was on the importance of integration it now seems to be on the value of self-help and of finding ways to express one's cultural identity.

The Indian

The Indians form the second largest group of immigrants to the United Kingdom and can generally be divided into two distinct occupational groups. Firstly there is the professional group which includes doctors, teachers, businessmen etc., and is distributed all over the United Kingdom. These 'professionals'

---

* The high proportion of West Indian mothers who work and the corresponding use of child minders is an important factor. This is one of the most striking and significant contrasts between West Indian and Asian families, and probably has a profound effect on the level and type of linguistic, cognitive and social development which many West Indian children have achieved on entry into the school system.

originate from all parts of India, many via East Africa. They speak English fluently and usually experience few problems of integration, although it is not uncommon to find that the wives of Indian 'professionals' are not nearly as fluent as their husbands in English. The second group, which is the largest, comprises the semi-skilled and the unskilled workers. The majority of the latter group originate from the rural Punjab and to a lesser degree from the Gujerat and the south. The mother tongue is Punjabi, Gujerati, Tamil or another Indian language. They do not usually speak English on arrival in Britain and some cannot speak it even after several years of residence in the United Kingdom. Their food is distinctively Indian, some being vegetarian. The men wear Western clothes while the women generally prefer their saris and salvars. In the case of the latter, Western dress and going out for work is the exception. The majority of Indians coming to this country are Hindus or Sikhs, with a Muslim and Christian minority. They have their own places of worship and keep their own religious festivals. Social activities are almost totally restricted to their own ethnic group. There is little mixing of sexes, and arranged marriages are common. Of the estimated 200,000 Indians living in Britain (1968) approximately 80 per cent were Sikhs and the remainder mostly Hindus.[10]

Like the West Indian system, the Indian educational system resembles the British one. Since 1961, eight or nine years of education has been compulsory through primary and secondary schools. It is only recently that free primary education has been available; yet about 70 per cent of the population remain illiterate. The system tends to suffer from 'a lack of trained teachers and slavish following of out-of-date methods'[10], which with the general lack of facilities and funds, prevent the solution of these problems. Additional difficulties reside in the diversity of languages in India: 'Primary schools function in the language of the area and teach Hindi as a foreign language. This [Hindi] becomes the medium of instruction at the next stage. English is

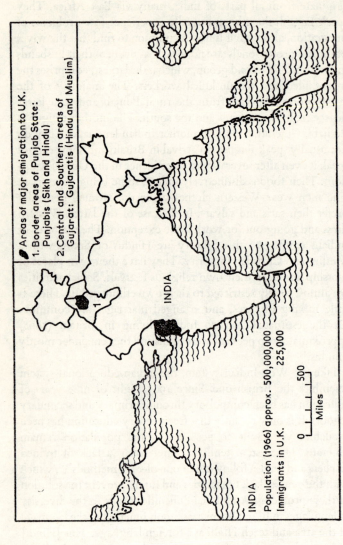

Fig. 2.2 *India: areas from which Indians have emigrated to the U.K. From I. Morrish, The Background of Immigrant Children, Unwin Educational Books, 1971.*

Areas of major emigration to U.K.
1. Border areas of Punjab State: Punjabis (Sikh and Hindu)
2. Central and Southern areas of Gujarat: Gujaratis (Hindu and Muslim)

INDIA

INDIA
Population (1966) approx. 500,000,000
Immigrants in U.K. 225,000

Miles
0   500

taught as a foreign language so that it can replace Hindi as a medium of further education in colleges and universities'.[10]

The typical West Indian and Asian family structures are both of the extended type, nevertheless there are clear differences between them. The West Indian extended family provides a stable background to the potentially unstable types of conjugal union most often found. Though contributing to the support and discipline of children even in stable concubinage, the extended family is most prominent in the event of this breaking down. The Asian extended family is a very important part of normal family life. It is centred on stable conjugal unions, and the various family members participate in the division of labour and fulfil traditional roles; they are crucial to the activities of the household. 'Land is held and farmed jointly on a co-operative basis . . . kitchens are communal, but there are separate sleeping quarters for each nuclear family or part. Family wealth is communally held and payments to individuals are made from the pooled resources'.[11]

These differences between West Indian and Indian family structure have become less marked in the British context as neither group has been able to maintain completely these forms of family organization, and each has tended to move towards the nuclear family structure.

It is interesting to note that in contrast to the West Indian situation the Indian father plays a very powerful role as an authoritarian figure. He must be conscientiously obeyed, and administers punishments to the children in later childhood. The mother is responsible for discipline during early childhood, the father often being a remote figure with little contact with the children at this stage. This strictness is much more prevalent in traditional rural families; in urban areas there is a tendency towards smaller households and more nuclear families, with less insistence on the traditional ways.

The Indian family is usually larger and more complex than the average British family and makes greater demands on each individual member. But it also offers them greater benefits. The individual Indian perceives himself surrounded not by concentric circles containing wives and children, close friends and acquaintances, but by his immediate family (which includes all his brothers and sisters as well as his own children), then by kin, including distant relatives, then by members of his village and finally by his linguistic group. His identification tends to be with, for example, other Punjabis rather than with Indians in general. Since many Indians are accustomed to living surrounded by kinsmen it is not surprising that they should attempt to recreate the same environment in Britain, setting up miniature Indian communities.

The organization of an Indian family is markedly different from that of a nuclear English family. Its head is the eldest male, normally the grandfather or, if he is dead, his eldest son. It is this man who makes all the major decisions. Therefore the head of many Indian families in Britain could live in India and what appears to be a family is actually a fraction of a 'joint' family still connected by a sort of umbilical cord to their country of origin. The whole scale of relationships in the Indian joint family is different from that in the typical British nuclear family. Whereas in Britain the responsibilities are divided between husband and wife, in India responsibilities are more widely spread among the family members, grandparents, other relatives, and often male children taking their share. The task of caring for aged parents is a responsibility which falls upon their sons, beginning with the eldest, and devolves upon the daughters, brothers, uncles, aunts and finally, if necessary, other relatives.

The place of a child in an Indian joint family is determined by its sex. Boys are an economic asset as potential wage-earners, and girls an economic liability because their parents must give any future husband's family a dowry upon marriage. Girls are discouraged from worldly experience and childhood is seen as an apprenticeship to becoming a competent, well-ordered housewife. On the other hand boys are given much more freedom as they grow older and are not expected to help in the home, their training being towards success in the outside world and masters in their own homes.

Both the duties and rights of each member in a joint family are carefully prescribed, everyone being fully aware of his/her own position. Discipline is the responsibility of both parents and generally Indian parents seem stricter than their English counterparts. However, the urbanization of India is gradually breaking up the traditional joint family, as changing economic conditions necessitate highly mobile family units leading to smaller, i.e. nuclear, families similar to those in Britain. In India the change is relatively slow but for the immigrant to this country the adjustment has to be more rapid and dramatic if he is to take full advantage of economic opportunities.

Obviously considerable difficulties and frustrations occur when the Indians in Britain attempt to imitate the nuclear family unit of their neighbours and simultaneously retain facets of a joint family. Of course the experience of the joint family can in fact be sufficient education in itself for the Indian child. However, in Britain many of the functions of the joint family have been taken over by the Welfare State and the school. It is not surprising that the school experience of many Indian children leads to a considerable amount of conflict with their parents.

The Pakistani

Pakistan was until 1972 a federal Islamic republic, formed from two widely-separated parts of the Indian sub-continent with a predominantly Moslem population: West and East Pakistan. West Pakistan is now Pakistan, and East Pakistan is the independent state of Bangladesh. These countries are separated by over 1,000 miles of Indian territory. Over half the population is concentrated in Pakistan, which is only one sixth of the area of Bangladesh. For the purposes of this section I shall consider both together, and not make any distinction between

B

Pakistanis and Bangladeshis. This is merely for convenience in discussing statistics, and is obviously not a distinction that can be ignored in any real sense.

The majority of Pakistani immigrants to this country originate from the northernmost borders of the two countries. In Pakistan the district of Mirpur in the Pakistani-held part of Kashmir is the source of much emigration, both historically and more recently. A similar situation obtains in the Sylhet district of Bangladesh. In addition the two areas have similar terrains, i.e. hilly and rocky, and in both one finds similar systems of agriculture, land tenure and family organization.

The Pakistani educational system retains the bias towards higher education that was the residue of white-centred British colonial rule. The greater proportion of available funds are assigned to the universities, the consequences of which being the illiteracy of the majority of the population, *viz.* 81 per cent over the age of five in 1961. This is also a reflection of the Pakistani view of the domestic role of children. The educational environment at home and at school is poverty-stricken: permanent school buildings are rare, discipline strict, and curricula inflexible, with considerable reliance on rote learning. A substantial proportion of immigrant fathers from the relatively prosperous Punjab have attended school for five years or more, but the vast majority of immigrants from the villages have had little or no formal education and are illiterate in their mother tongue.

The Pakistanis are the closest knit group of immigrants in the United Kingdom. Like the Indians there is a small group of Pakistani professional people in this country. The large unskilled and semi-skilled group originates from the Punjab, Bengal and Azad Kashmir. A very large proportion of the married men have left their families behind; indeed the number of married men living alone is highest among the Pakistanis. The men wear Western dress but the women keep to their traditional costumes. Sexual segregation is strict and communication across sexes rare, women rarely being allowed out to

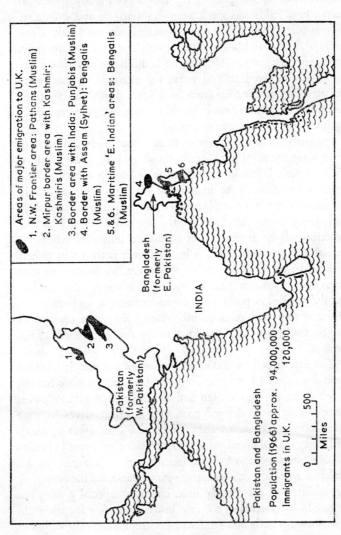

Fig. 2.3 *Pakistan and Bangladesh: Areas from which Pakistanis have emigrated to the UK. Adapted from: I. Morrish, The Background of Immigrant Children, Unwin Educational Books, 1971.*

Areas of major emigration to U.K.

1. N.W. Frontier area: Pathans (Muslim)
2. Mirpur border area with Kashmir: Kashmiris (Muslim)
3. Border area with India: Punjabis (Muslim)
4. Border with Assam (Sylhet): Bengalis (Muslim)
5. & 6. Maritime 'E. Indian' areas: Bengalis (Muslim)

Bangladesh (formerly E. Pakistan)

INDIA

Pakistan (formerly W. Pakistan)

Pakistan and Bangladesh
Population (1966) approx. 94,000,000
Immigrants in U.K. 120,000

0   500
Miles

work. Urdu or Bengali are the languages usually spoken at home. Few Pakistanis speak English on arrival and even after several years English is spoken with difficulty and only when essential. They are Muslim by religion, have their own mosques and keep their own religious festivals. Religious rituals are rigorously adhered to and pork, for example, is not eaten. Usually they prefer their own food, see Indian/Pakistani films and listen to Eastern music. Social interaction is almost totally limited to their own ethnic group.

For the Pakistani migrant to Britain the family and kinship groups are the focal point of almost all areas of social conduct. This extended family crosses over several generations and extends horizontally to include all the male descendants in the father's line in a complex pattern of reciprocal relationships and obligations. Underlying the extended family is the function of the family as an economic unit and when the available work in Pakistan is insufficient it is then that fathers and sons may be sent further afield, e.g. to Britain, to find alternative opportunities. In such circumstances the 'nuclear family' is always potentially dependent on the support of the larger group and consequently strong sanctions operate to subject the will of the individual to the collective needs of the group.

The activities in a Pakistani household are clearly divided between men and women the latter being responsible for the care of the young children and all domestic duties. Women have very clearly defined roles and in effect wives become contractual servants to their husbands. The father's role is primarily that of bread-winner and he takes little part in household management, often remaining a remote figure to his children especially in their early years. Because of the economic significance of the family unit, children, especially sons, are regarded by parents as the best insurance policy for their old age. Consequently the family places emphasis on the religious and social training of the child, on discipline to the will of the parents, and on the fulfilment of responsibilities with the extended family.

As yet there are few apparent changes in the life styles of the Pakistani family in Britain probably because the gradual arrival of women coming to join their husbands and sons has tended to strengthen the traditional codes of conduct. In this respect many an adolescent boy now finds himself living in what his English peers would regard as a 'normal' family now that his mother has joined them. However, in view of the segregation of the sexes in Pakistani households her arrival will have little effect upon the boy's life in the male family.

Pakistani parents place considerable value upon their children's education, for they hope that it will lead to an increase in the family's status, and they see themselves as instrumental in ensuring that their children apply themselves fully to their school work. Regarding their daughter's education they find themselves in an ambivalent position. Although the parents realize that education will assist their daughters in acquiring good husbands they are concerned that education in a mixed English school may result in the girls developing aspirations incompatible with their expected roles as wives. Pakistani girls (similarly to Indian girls) are thus placed in a position of considerable stress between the conflicting demands of home and English school. In such situations parents may try to assert their values by reinforcing their authority over their children through stricter discipline in the home.

Since discipline in Pakistani homes is generally strict parents may well disapprove of the relatively permissive treatment of their children at school, which they perceive as a threat to their ability to demand unquestioning obedience from their children. In this respect many of the Pakistanis who have been in Britain for a number of years are very concerned that their children's adherence to traditional codes of behaviour is being undermined as a result of different attitudes and values promulgated by British schools. Accordingly many Pakistani communities in

Britain have made provision for formal religious and cultural instruction for their children to counter what they perceive as a real danger in English society, i.e. complete assimilation for their ethnic group and the resultant loss of identity.

This chapter has attempted to give an overview of the largest minority ethnic groups living in the United Kingdom i.e. West Indian, Indian and Pakistani. I realize the constrictions inherent in such a task but would anticipate that the reader who wishes to pursue further study will find the references useful. I hope it has been of some help to identify some of the factors appertaining to the three minority ethnic groups which make them distinct from indigenous pupils and which could possibly affect their learning in British schools. These factors must be borne in mind when reading the chapters which follow.

References

1 SMITH, M. G. (1965) *The Plural Society in the British West Indies*. University of California Press.

2 HERSKOVITS, M. J. & F. E. (1964) *Trinidad Village*. New York: Octagon Books.

3 HENRIQUES, F. (1953) *Family and colour in Jamaica*. Eyre & Spottiswoode.

4 ROSE, E. J. B., DEAKIN, N. *et al.* (1969) *Colour and Citizenship: A Report on British Race Relations*. Oxford University Press/Institute of Race Relations.

5 NETTLEFOLD, R. (1965) National identity and attitude to race in Jamaica. *Race* **7**, 1, 59–72.

6 BENTLEY, S. (1970) Black power and abeng. *Race Today* **2**, 2, 50–2.

7 HILL, D. (1973) The attitudes of ethnic minorities in Britain among adolescents. Unpub. PhD thesis, University of Birmingham.

8 BHATNAGAR, J. K. (1970) *Immigrants at School*. Cornmarket Press.

9 BELL, R. R. (1969) The lower class Negro family in the United States and Great Britain. *Race* **11,** 2.
10 BELL, R. (1968) The Indian background. In R. Oakley (ed.) *New Backgrounds.* Oxford University Press/Institute of Race Relations.
11 BOWKER, G. (1968) *The Education of Coloured Immigrants.* Longman.

3

Assessment
of ability and
attainment

There have been very few researches on the educational needs
and responses of pupils from minority ethnic groups but the
recent surveys conducted by the Inner London Education
Authority indicate that urgent attention in this area is required.
First a literacy survey was made of pupils who were beginning
their second year of primary education. This revealed a considerable discrepancy between the performance of pupils from
minority ethnic groups and that of the indigenous population:
14.8 per cent of indigenous and 28.5 per cent of minority
ethnic groups were defined as 'poor' readers. The same survey
also looked at the number of 'good' readers and suggested that
there were four times as many indigenous pupils in this category
as those from minority ethnic groups (i.e. 12 per cent as opposed
to 3 per cent).

In 1971 subsequent research in the same area indicated that 'as
in the previous survey immigrants' attainment was on average
markedly lower than that of non-immigrants', the mean reading
age for the former group being at least a year below
that of the indigenous pupils. The survey team also found
evidence that, at the end of their primary education, twice as

many pupils from minority ethnic groups than would be expected by chance are located at the lower end of the performance distribution and only about one third are found in the upper streams. However, such results are open to wide interpretation. What is more significant perhaps is that these surveys also show that pupils from minority ethnic groups who have been born in Britain and fully educated in this country are still underfunctioning in primary schools compared with their indigenous counterparts.[1] Of course the low performance of minority ethnic group pupils is an important factor in their placement in lower ability classes, particularly in the secondary schools where streaming is retained. In this respect a survey[2] by the NFER showed that West Indian, Indian and Pakistani children were frequently found in the bottom streams. It is rather disturbing to note that of the 230 multiracial schools surveyed only *one* reported that West Indian, Indian and Pakistani pupils were frequently placed in the higher streams. In fact this school was referring specifically to pupils of Indian origin; and a few other schools reported that Indians and Pakistanis were to be found in their middle streams. In addition the NFER survey found that although this pattern of 'low stream placement' coupled with low performance applied throughout the English educational system, a larger proportion of minority ethnic group pupils remain at school for fifth and sixth form courses compared to indigenous pupils, but following courses at a lower level such as CSE or O Level. When considering A levels the proportions were reversed, i.e. there was a much smaller proportion of pupils from minority ethnic groups taking these courses than indigenous pupils. In this respect it was reported that only one in five West Indian sixth formers was pursuing such a course, and the proportion of Asian pupils was only fractionally higher.[2] Obviously urgent attention and action is needed to prevent a deterioration in this situation. Another NFER project[3] has indicated some ways in which many teachers are successfully adapting their curricula, but this report also revealed that a much larger group of teachers were doing nothing at all in this direction. A report, *Teacher Education for a Multi-Cultural Society*, published jointly by the CRC and ATCDE (1974), referring to the above had this to say; 'If large numbers of these pupils continue to fail significantly to realise their potential and only a small minority achieve their aspirations, a substantial part of the population identified by the colour of its skin will be performing at a level below that of other groups. Employment prospects for such a group are unlikely to be good and may well be worsening, as economic change brings with it a declining demand for semi-skilled and un-skilled work in particular and manual work in general. The danger is that we may produce a lower class, either unemployed or only able to do the most menial work, which will easily be distinguished by its colour. The situation already exists in other countries and the effects are plain to see. All concerned with good race relations would wish to avoid this, and it can be, but the educational system must play its part and only adequate training can ensure this.' This is not to say that all minority ethnic group children are failing at school. There is evidence that some teachers and some schools have successfully tackled the challenge of teaching these children, but this is too small a minority.

A major problem of assessment in multiracial schools has been that most of the traditional tests are culturally loaded against minority ethnic groups in several ways e.g. they make no allowance for language difficulties, lack of familiarity with the subject matter or the form of testing. Relating to the latter it has been proved that, for example, the colour of the tester can adversely affect a child's score although perhaps this effect, probably extreme when the children first enter our school system, gradually lessens as they become more accustomed to their new country.

Obviously if the purpose of the tests is to assess the pupil's level of functioning at a particular time, then they might be useful diagnostic instruments. But if they are used to establish attainment as a basis for dividing a group of children into streams, or to forecast future levels of attainment then these tests, or indeed any form of teacher assessment with the same end in view, can place immigrant pupils at a distinct disadvantage. What then have been and are schools procedures for assessing children from minority ethnic groups? The NFER study, *Organization in Multi-Racial Schools*,[2] investigated this area and their results have been incorporated into this chapter. Concerning tests of ability, many primary and secondary schools apply these to both minority ethnic groups and indigenous pupils alike. Surveys have shown that a list of such tests would include almost every test available. However, headteachers have been generally aware of the shortcomings of such instruments, justifying their use only if used in conjunction with teacher reports and opinions and if the child's knowledge of the English language was deemed sufficient.

Concerning tests of attainment many primary and proportionately less secondary schools have used these for minority ethnic group and indigenous pupils. The most popular tests have been English, Mathematics and Verbal Reasoning, with English tests being favoured most. The Burt and Schonell Graded Word Reading Tests are popular and many schools have applied such tests at regular intervals e.g. annually or every six months. Other tests which examine a greater range of English skills than merely word recognition have been used and include, for example, NFER, Schonell, Holborn, Daniells and Diack, and Neale.

Other methods of assessment in schools include:

1 Progress through a reading scheme (especially primary).
2 Written essay-type examination (especially secondary).
3 Written examination with short answers (especially secondary).
4 Teacher assessment. This category includes discussion

amongst staff of pupils' progress and general impression-istic evaluation.

From the foregoing it is obvious that most schools have adapted to subjective assessment and accepted that in the absence of specially prepared tests for multiracial schools the most valuable form of assessment relies very heavily on the judgement of experienced teachers.

An unpopular idea related to the assessment of minority ethnic group pupils is that some form of special allowances for their difficulties should be devised. This attitude is also reported in the Department of Education and Science Education Survey 10: *Potential and Progress in a Second Culture*[4], (1971) which states:

> 'Many secondary schools are well aware of a conflict of principle with regard to assessment. On the one hand the normal pattern of internal and external examinations does not discriminate between groups of pupils except in relation to attainment in the subjects concerned. But it is recognized that these methods do not do justice to the potential and, indeed, the knowledge of many immigrant children. On the other hand special methods to assess their progress may, it is said, suggest discrimination on ethnic grounds and may create a sense of second-class citizenship.'

A headteacher quoted in Townsend and Brittan,[2] who would clearly support the above statement, put the point thus: 'Some allowance may be made for any immigrant pupil with language difficulty, but the whole aim of the school is gradually to treat all pupils alike be they immigrant or non-immigrant. This is in preparation for leaving school and entry into employment and the adult world. The immigrant pupil is made aware of the advantage to him of language mastery to help him compete on equal terms with other people. This they appreciate and readily act on, looking for no preferential treatment in school, but are always ready to ask for any help they may need.'

The DES report was based on the findings of a pilot survey carried out in 1969 by a number of HM Inspectorate in ten local education authorities into current practice and opinion on the assessment of pupils from overseas. It suggests that many teachers are confused by recent research into questions of intelligence, ability and potential and how these can be assessed. Much of the work done in these fields is not well known to teachers and a tendency still exists for them to 'think of a level of ability fixed for each individual and to rely on professional experience to judge it'. The report recognizes that many of the conventional ways of examining and testing are culturally loaded against minority ethnic group children. Even a simple reading comprehension test 'may reveal misunderstandings of concepts and situations which may bear little relation to the reading difficulty of the material or the reading competence of the immigrant.'

In most authorities, according to the report, assessment in infant and junior schools was by the subjective judgement of the class teacher although often graded word reading tests were used. Some teachers were dissatisfied with these tests, since the mechanical reading skills of minority ethnic group pupils were often ahead of their comprehension. At the time of transfer to secondary schools it was standard procedure in most of the authorities surveyed for all pupils to take tests in verbal reasoning, English and arithmetic although, according to the report, 'it was generally recognized that these procedures often had little relevance for immigrant pupils of all kinds'.

On arrival at the secondary school many minority ethnic group pupils were graded according to the same standards as all other pupils and placed in the appropriate stream or ability band. More recent arrivals were sometimes placed in special language groups and in some schools in remedial departments with slow learning local children. Whilst in the special language groups much attention was paid to the development of the pupil's language and care was usually taken to decide on the right time for transfer to an ordinary class. This was frequently to a class one or two years below the pupil's age group. However, it must be said that the pressure of numbers of incoming pupils into the special language groups has often defeated the best intentions, and therefore these groups have not always been as effective in practice as in intention. Once in an ordinary class the pupils were assessed by procedures which took no account of their special language needs. In some cases problems with language might go largely undetected until the time when the immigrant pupils passed GCE in several technical subjects but failed in English. Many teachers recognized that the normal patterns of internal and external examinations did not do justice to the abilities and often to the knowledge of their minority ethnic group pupils and said they would welcome an examination for immigrant school leavers on the lines of the West Midlands area CSE examination in English as a second language.

The report also considered whether it would be advisable to develop tests specifically for use with minority ethnic group pupils and concluded that 'there would appear to be a significant body of opinion which would hope that any methods of assessment developed might be of use with a wider range of pupils than immigrants, and that such methods might have some long term application in identifying the problems of children whose social, cultural and linguistic backgrounds may make it difficult for them to respond to conventional forms of education.' Culture-fair tests, the report maintained, are now recognized as difficult to devise in practice, even if possible theoretically, and of doubtful value in schools even then. It would also seem that it is in the field of language development and proficiency in English that there is most demand for appropriate methods of assessment. Teachers experienced in second-language teaching were able to make these assessments with confidence but teachers not involved in this work usually had difficulties in making judgements about the immigrant pupil's skill in English.

Amongst the report's conclusions is a recommendation that 'high priority should continue to be given to the development of means by which the ordinary class teacher can assess and be made aware of progress made by the immigrant pupils in acquiring a second language, in particular a functional proficiency in English adequate for secondary education.'

It seems fairly clear from the foregoing that in multiracial schools a considerable amount of assessment is based upon instruments that have been developed over many years for a vastly different school population. Teachers understand that these tests are of limited validity in the present multiracial context and evidence indicates that subjective modifications are made in interpretation if not in application. As previously mentioned, many schools no longer use published tests because of their deficiencies, preferring to use subjective assessments based largely on teacher expertise and knowledge of individual pupils. These methods only have validity in the school in which they are used and teacher expectation is likely to have distorting effects in a situation where the effects in a situation where the effects of poor linguistic competence interfere with the assessment of educational attainment.

In such a situation it would appear that two solutions are possible; (i) the development of new batteries of objective tests suitable for use in all multiracial schools and (ii) the improvement of teachers' subjective assessments, which though useful run into difficulties where reliability and validity are concerned. Work on the former has already been done. For example, Dr Haynes (1971)[5] at the National Foundation of Educational Research has developed new learning ability tests which are geared to a specific cultural group and which have been shown to be good predictors of the performance of the children in that group. These new tests include tests of verbal learning, reasoning ability and concept formation, using concrete materials which do not require a knowledge of the English language. The tests were tried out over a two-year period on 125 Punjabi speaking children in Ealing junior schools.

Dr Haynes also gave the children traditional tests of intelligence and attainment and compared the results of these, and teachers' estimates of the children's ability, with the results of the learning ability tests. It was found that teachers' estimates of the children's ability were efficient but the new learning ability tests were even better predictors of performance, and certainly far better than the present intelligence tests. Teachers' estimates of the ability of Indian children were, incidentally, slightly less efficient than their estimates of English children's ability. These new tests are currently only suitable for individual application by educational psychologists and are obviously not of much assistance to the teacher. However, they are being developed so that they may have wider usage.

Concerning the improvement of teachers' subjective assessments the following is an example suggested by the Birmingham EPA Project (1974)[6] on the assessment of oral language. This is also quoted in P. Widlake, *The Multiracial Class* (Evans, 1973):

Assessment: Oral Language

It is not difficult to draw up a simple, standard interview form, so that after receiving a few non-English speaking children, the teacher will have some idea of how their language compares with others. Some local authorities have specialist language teachers to help in this work, but young teachers may find themselves without such assistance.

Having noted the child's name, sex, guardian, address and date of birth, record his or her responses to:

1 Simple basic questions: What is your name? Where do you live? How many fingers? (holding up 1–5)

2 Imperatives: Give me a pencil. Shut the door.
3 Colours: Show me the blue pencil (displaying a blue and green pencil).
4 Prepositions. Place a book on the table or hold it under the table. Ask: Where is the book?
5 Time.

Boys and girls at a more advanced standard may be assessed on:

6 Comparatives: The blue pencil is long, but the red pencil is——
Superlatives: long, longer, longest.
7 Changes of tense:
Rajinder is writing. Yesterday Rajinder——
Tomorrow Rajinder—— ——

Children whose English is more advanced may comprehend much more than they express. This is, in fact, characteristic of second language users. As soon as they have gained enough confidence to begin using their language, the teacher can try to record examples of particular sentence patterns. Text-books like Papadopoulos, *English Now* (Longman) or the Schools Council's scope handbook (Longman) place the sentence patterns in a sequence. For example, *English Now* teaches patterns in the following order:

What is it? It's a——
Is it a——? Yes, it is. No it isn't.
Is it a—— or a ——?
What colour is it?
My. It's my cap.
Your. It's your bag, etc.

A little study will enable the teacher to assemble these teaching sequences into a rough and ready assessment procedure.

As a further example of teachers' subjective assessments here is one used by the Crown Street Language Centre in Liverpool. This report has two main functions: (i) As a progress report on pupils who have attended lessons in English as a second language at the Centre; (ii) As a check list for assisting teachers in ordinary schools when pupils are unable to attend the language centre. It should also be noted that a set of supplementary cards are used to illustrate certain features of the report.

Progress Report on Lessons in English as a Second Language

Name of pupil:

Home address:

Mother tongue: School:

Previous schools (abroad and in UK):

Date of birth: Date of arrival in UK:

Dates of attendance at lessons in English as a second language:

Others in family:

General comments (behaviour, ability to mix etc.):

Level of English language (the appropriate numbers are ringed):

Listening

4 Understands different kinds of English well.

3 Can follow a story or set of instructions within restricted vocabulary.

2 Limited to simple instructions.

1 Understands only the odd word.

Speaking

4 Speaks fluently in all situations.

3 Can hold a conversation or retell a story within restricted vocabulary.

2 Can use only simple sentences.

1 Limited to a few words, e.g., numbers, names of common objects.

Reading
4 Capable of reading widely.
3 Understands a short story within a restricted vocabulary.
2 Can read only familiar sentences.
1 Recognizes only a few words.

Writing
4 Can do free composition work, e.g. diary, essays.
3 Can do controlled composition work.
2 Can write only simple exercises, e.g. completing sentences.
1 Can only copy a few words.

Further comments on language.

Grammatical structures covered in lessons. A tick against an item indicates that the pupil should be familiar with it.

Structure	*Examples*
1 *Articles (a, an, the, some, any, no)*	What's this? It's *a* car/*an* aeroplane/*the* sun. I want *some* milk/I haven't *any* Who's that? It's Mr. Smith.
2 *Personal pronouns*	I, me, you, he, etc.
3 *Present tense of be, have, can, must* (+*negative and interrogative*)	I am I'm not Am I? There is There isn't Is there? I have I haven't Have I? I can I can't Can I?
4 *Present continuous of other verbs*	What's he *doing*? He's reading.
5 *Possessives*	Who*se* book is it? It's John*s*/ *my* book/*mine*
6 *Prepositions*	Where's the pencil? It's *in*/*on*/ *under* the desk.
7 *Plurals*	What are these? They're cat*s*/ dog*s*/buse*s*

8 *Cardinal numbers, money*	How many pens are there? There are *10* pens
	How much money have you? I have *25p*
9 *Ordinal numbers, dates, days, months*	What's the date? It's the *fifth of October.*
Telling the time.	What's the time? It's *ten past five.*
10 *Colours, shapes*	What colour/shape is it? It's *blue/square*
11 *Adjective + noun*	Which book? *The red book.*
12 *Comparison of adjectives*	Bigger *than/as* big *as/the* biggest.
13 *Simple present*	He gets up. He doesn't get up. Does he get up?
14 *Future with*	
(*a*) 'going to'	What are you going to do? *I'm going to* write.
(*b*) 'shall/will'	When *will* you *see* him? *I'll see* him tomorrow.
15 *Simple past, regular and irregular*	What did you buy yesterday? I bought some ——
	Clean*ed*, post*ed*, work*ed* saw, went, thought.
16 *Present perfect*	*I have* wash*ed*, clean*ed*; *I have* seen, bought.

N.B. These are the basic grammatical structures introduced in most elementary textbooks of English as a second language. They can be used for revision and for new work. The important point is that the structures should be practised in sentences and in situations – as suggested in the above examples – and not in isolation.

Teacher's signature   Date

Types of assessment like the above are suitable for classroom use, and help fulfil the need expressed in the DES's 1971 report; 'There is a need to distinguish between standardized tests and methods of assessment which may take a long time to develop and less sophisticated means by which a teacher can check the progress of his pupils and determine their needs. Projects to develop the latter kind of assessment should be given priority.'

In addition to these local assessment methods, new tests[7] are now available for assessing the language proficiency of children who speak English as a second language or have a dialect variant. The tests have been designed by the National Foundation for Educational Research and are suitable for classroom use. They are intended for children of junior age and can also be used with native English speakers. The tests have three main functions:

1 They can help teachers with placement, in special language classes, in deciding whether extra tuition is necessary or whether pupils are ready to return to normal classes.
2 They can give teachers specific linguistic information for each child tested, which can be used for diagnostic purposes.
3 They can help teachers to monitor progress.

Tests used by teachers usually give norm tables but in the case of these tests such tables would be of little practical help to the teacher, who needs to know how to translate the test scores into teaching terms. Scores on the tests are therefore reported in relation to the content and the skills measured.

The linguistic framework within which the test material has been constructed is one in which language is viewed as a set of skills. At the grossest level, the skills are those of listening, speaking, reading and writing. Each of these skills may be said to involve a number of component skills, which may be arranged in ascending levels of sophistication and complexity so that each level incorporates and assumes all previous levels. The gross skills are analysed into sets of component skills.

The skills involved in listening, for instance, are listed as follows:

(i) Discriminating the sounds of English.
(ii) Recognizing and understanding spoken English words.
(iii) Understanding (lexically and syntactically) well-formed spoken English statements, questions and instructions.
(iv) Following and understanding an extended piece of spoken English: exposition, argument, description, etc.
(v) Responding approximately to significant variation in the spoken language, (this involves, for instance, the ability to perceive the level of formality of a situation mainly from the language used, and the ability to behave accordingly.)

Speaking, reading and writing are similarly dealt with and all the listening and reading tests are of the multiple choice answer type. The writing and speaking tests are open-ended and intelligibility is the criterion for scoring. The speaking tests are individually administered, the other tests are not. The Teacher's Guide describes ways of interpreting the tests:

The overall score of a child on a particular test will indicate his general level of competence in the area covered by the test. For many of the tests, however, it may prove to be more useful to take a more qualitative view of the child's performance and to consider his responses to specific items in terms of the grammatical content of the items. For this purpose a list of the grammatical points tested by specific items is given in Appendix One in the Guide. This analytical approach will prove more helpful at some levels than at others. At Level One, for example, where only a single word is tested, the grammatical content of an item will consist simply of the part of speech of the word tested. However, in the following two levels, where an item involves a whole sentence, the grammatical feature incorporated in the item will be the relation of one part of speech to another, and it is here that an analysis of responses might be particularly helpful. Where more extended pieces of speech or writing are involved, a consideration of specific errors may be less appropriate and, in general, for Level Three, it is the overall score on the test which is important. However, in the items consisting of stories followed by questions in Level Three listening and reading, the answer choices for some of the questions have been constructed to test the ability to distinguish between one form of question and another and it is worth giving special attention therefore, to the responses to these particular questions. Details of the question forms tested at this level are also to be found in Appendix One.

The *Teacher's Guide* goes on to give detailed information on interpreting the results of each section of the tests, and contains appendices on the linguistic content of the tests and test statistics.

Summary

Unfortunately by general consensus, the financial backing for research and development in the assessment of ability and attainment in multiracial schools has not been available. Consequently many schools use traditional tests, often where the use of such instruments is neither valid nor reliable, and as a result many pupils can and have been misplaced in schools where they are among low-achievers and are given little motivation to progress. Their attendance at such a school may put them at a life-long disadvantage.

The teacher obviously needs instruments like those used in Birmingham (p. 40) and Liverpool (p. 42), which can be used regularly in the classroom to assess progress and diagnose difficulties. There is a particular need for these tests when pupils arrive from overseas, or when they are transferred back to school from language centres.

It would seem an almost impossible task to devise a range of measures which could be standardized in multiracial schools of necessarily varying kinds. A solution would seem to lie in improving the quality of school-based assessments. This presupposes that the teacher's professional expertise would also need to be improved. Assuming this is attained, the outcome would be measures geared more to the particular individual or group, and the benefit of such a development would be harvested in fields beyond that of multiracial education.

A selected list of studies related to the assessment of ability and attainment

The following five studies are all mentioned in *Immigrants at School* by J. K. Bhatnagar (Cornmarket Press, 1970):

CRAIG (1963)
English children were significantly superior to Jamaican children in linguistic ability, especially those aspects of linguistic ability which correlated highly with 'g' factor (general ability).

SAINT (1963)
(a) IQ of immigrant children was found to be 15 points below the national mean.
(b) Attainment of these children was poor.
(c) IQ showed a positive correlation with the length of residence in the UK.

HOUGHTON (1966)
Little difference was found between the mean IQ of English and Jamaican infants.

WILES (1968)
(a) Immigrant children who had full range of primary education in this country had a higher attainment than English children.
(b) Those who did not have their primary education in Britain did considerably worse than others.

LITTLE *et al.* (1969)

(a) The attainment of immigrant children was worse than that of English children though an improvement with the increased length of stay was noticed.

(b) West Indian performance was the worst among the immigrant groups.

(c) There was no difference between the academic attainment of English children in schools with high and low proportions of immigrants.

WATSON, P. (1973) Stability of IQ of immigrant and non-immigrant slow-learning pupils. *Brit. Journal of Educational Psychology* **43,** 1, 80–2.

A group of West Indian children suspected by teachers to be slow learners were tested on the Wechler Verbal Intelligence Scale for Children. Those who scored less than 80 were retested two years later. The mean rise in IQ among these children was eight points. A control group of non-immigrant pupils of similar ability was reassessed after a similar period, the mean rise in this case was only .25 of a point.

VERNON, P. E. (1965) Environmental handicaps and intellectual development, II. *Brit. Journal of Educational Psychology* **35,** 117–26.

Stated that the most predictive instrument for West Indian immigrants is the Verbal Wechsler Intelligence Scale for Children, provided that the children are old enough and it is given by a tester with some familiarity with West Indian speech. Found performance tests less suitable.

MCFIE, I. and THOMPSON, J. A. (1970) Intellectual abilities of immigrant children. *Brit. Journal of Educational Psychology* **40,** 348–51.

Concluded that a group of West Indian immigrants whom they studied were at a greater disadvantage on performance problems than they were on verbal ones.

TAYLOR, J. H. (1973) Newcastle upon Tyne: Asian pupils

do better than Whites. *Brit. Journal of Sociology* **24**, 4, 431–447.

Taylor found in his research in Newcastle that Indian and Pakistani youths who came to England young did indeed achieve more educationally than late arrivals. However, in sharp contrast to all these other students Taylor shows that these young men did better overall than a matched sample of English boys in the same schools. In his article, which contains a detailed analysis of research in this area, he refers to the fact that almost all previous research on the performance of coloured immigrant pupils in English schools shows them either to be concentrated in the lower streams, or to do less well academically, than English children, or to score lower on intelligence tests – or at least to score well below the norm of the test. The only exception to this pattern is Houghton's findings (see above) that there was no significant difference to the test scores of two matched groups of West Indian and English infant pupils, both from deprived backgrounds. The best any of the other investigations can establish is a positive association between the coloured children's performance and the length of their English schooling, so that when they have had a complete English education their achievement is much the same as that of English children, 'if not slightly better'.

References

1 *Educational Needs of Children from Minority Groups*. Community Relations Commission, 1974.
2 TOWNSEND, H. E. R. and BRITTAN, E. (1972) *Organization in Multiracial Schools*. Slough: NFER.
3 TOWNSEND, H. E. R. and BRITTAN, E. (1973) *Multiracial Education: Needs and Innovation*. Schools Council Working Paper 50. Evans/Methuen Educational.
4 DES (1971) *Potential and Progress in a Second Culture: A survey of the assessment of pupils from overseas*. HMSO.

5 HAYNES, J. M. (1971) *Educational Assessment of Immigrant Pupils*. NFER.
6 BARNES, JACK (ed.) (1974) *EPA: Evaluated Action in London and Birmingham*, Volume 3 of the Educational Priority Area Publications. DES and Social Science Research Council.
7 NFER (1973) *English Proficiency Tests*. Aylesbury: Ginn.

4

Language difficulties

It is true that in most areas in Britain today there are few new arrivals of children from abroad, but this does not mean that language difficulties, and in particular the problems of teaching English to both immigrant and native-born children belonging to minority ethnic groups, have diminished. On the contrary we now have a clearer and more realistic view concerning the nature of such difficulties and, what is more important, it is generally recognized that there is no speedy solution. Many of the children, especially those whose language deficiencies have attracted most attention so far, need to learn English as a completely new language, i.e. as a second language. Most of these children have come to this country direct from India, Pakistan, Bangladesh and Cyprus, although there are also small, yet significant, groups from Portugal, Hong Kong, Yemen and elsewhere. Once it was believed that non-English speaking immigrant children would soon 'pick up' the English language without special help, but this notion is now discredited. An equally important group of learners, much neglected until the past five years, is that of children of West Indian origin whose Creole dialect is frequently very different from the dialects spoken by other pupils, teachers, and the indigenous local community. Such a difference, as mentioned later, has been a major source of educational difficulty for these pupils.

The varied home backgrounds of the children, the language they use at home, their parents' expectations of school, are just a few of the many factors which affect the way they react to school and to English, the language which holds the key to so many doors of future learning.

For many of these children it is only at school that they have the chance to use English and it is therefore essential that their repertoire of vocabulary and language structures should constantly be developed and extended. (This point will be further developed in this chapter.)

The demand for materials for teaching English as a second language overseas has produced a large selection of graded language practice books and other teaching aids. Many of these are unfamiliar to British teachers, but the National Book League publication, *English for Immigrant Children* (edited by June Derrick), provides an admirable review of the work in this, and associated, areas. Much of the material described in this book is used with school children (often indigenous) as the basis of their normal language work. It is up to the teacher to choose or adapt schemes which are appropriate to the particular needs of his/her pupils.

For the teacher approaching this topic for the first time, the amount of available material is overwhelming, and my aim in this chapter is to provide a selective review of the relevant literature, focussing upon major factors in language difficulties and setting these in the appropriate context. All the language materials mentioned have been used successfully in multiracial schools and it is anticipated that the section will offer some guidance to those teachers who find themselves in this situation for the first time and are unaware of available support. I have concentrated upon West Indian and Asian pupils since these represent the two largest minority ethnic groups in Britain and serve best to illustrate the kinds of difficulties that can arise in the classroom.

West Indian pupils

The 'interference' which the teacher can expect in the English of an immigrant West Indian child from his Creole vernacular will occur at all levels; i.e. phonological, morphological, syntactic and semantic. At the phonological level the words are not pronounced in the same way as in Standard English, and there is therefore no difference in Jamaican English between the pronunciation of words like 'hat' and 'hot'. At the morphological level, there is no inflection for plural or for tense in Creole:* di pus – *the cat*, di tuu puss – *the two cats*. At the syntactical level a very good illustration is provided by the phrase di biebi niem rabat – *The baby's name* (or, *the baby is named*) Robert. Here 'niem' can be regarded, if we wish to impose on the sentence the kind of syntactical divisions which we would apply to English, as either a noun or a verb; but in fact by labelling it in this manner we are imposing on the Creole structure a division which is not inherent in it.

Therefore we must say that there are two completely different systems: the structural system of the Creole and that of English. If one possesses no knowledge of the structure of the Creole and has had no sort of introduction to linguistics one might be tempted to dismiss what is referred to in Jamaica as 'bad talk' or 'African talk', and insist on the pupils speaking what is known as 'proper English'. The West Indian pupil will probably spot that there are a number of correspondences between the 'proper' English and Creole vernacular. Accordingly he may try to make a composite system out of what he knows and

* This method of writing the Jamaican dialect is one used by linguists and not by the dialect speakers themselves. Those readers who would like to discover more about West Indian dialect should read *Jamaica Talk* by I. G. Cassidy (Cambridge University Press, 1967).

understands well and the 'proper' English. Obviously the resultant single system will be an artificial one in which 'proper' or 'correct' English becomes something to be obtained if educational and social advancement is to be achieved. In such a situation education itself will become something very alien to these pupils.

However, on a more optimistic note, if teachers can be trained to be aware of these difficulties and accept the Creole vernacular as a language similar to any other, then he or she can suggest to his pupils that they should think of Creole as the language they speak in their homes where it is ideally suited. However, he must also emphasize that if they wish to be understood in the wider community then it will be to their advantage to master the 'proper' English. One of the greatest problems here is giving teachers time to gain the necessary knowledge. If the teachers are aware of the Creole structure then they will appreciate the difficulties the pupils are experiencing; e.g. some cannot hear the difference between some English phonemes because the phonemic contrasts are different in Creole, and it is more common to hear those differences of sound which are phonemically distinctive in our language.

It is possible to describe with considerable accuracy the linguistic behaviour of West Indian pupils but there is also the psychological aspect which must be understood and taken into account. For many years parts of the Caribbean have invested 'psychological' capital into acquiring 'proper'/'correct' English as a passport to economic and social advancement. Clearly, then most West Indians will resent the inference that such an investment is mistaken and will find it hard to acknowledge that the link between mastering proper English and economic and social advancement obtained only when a minority 'elite' were receiving secondary education, but is an inappropriate connection to make these days when secondary education is available to all. One of the results of failing to obtain the expected advancement through English education is resentment and a desire to revenge oneself on the system. As this can lead to behaviour of anti-social sort, it is important to try and encourage a more realistic attitude to the benefits of education right from the start. The same inflated expectations of education lie behind the pressure to succeed at school which is often put on West Indian pupils by their parents: and indeed behind the resentment which the parents might feel if told that their child needs special or remedial tuition.

West Indian pupils and CONCEPT 7–9

In 1967 the Schools Council Project for teaching English to West Indian children was established at Birmingham University to investigate and produce materials to remedy the particular language difficulties experienced by these children. The materials produced by the project are now published by E. J. Arnold and are available under the title CONCEPT 7–9.

Fig. 4.1 *A page from the Activity Book for use with Unit Two on concept building.* CONCEPT 7–9 (*published by E. J. Arnold*).

Although the Schools Council project set out initially to develop materials for teaching English to West Indian children, the team discovered that many of the materials they had developed were appropriate for more general use with children – but particularly those who were socially or educationally disadvantaged. The materials have been designed to help children develop skills which underlie success with language.

The final published materials consist of three units and a special dialect kit for West Indian children.

Unit One, Listening with Understanding aims to increase the pupils' skills of oral comprehension. In this unit the language becomes more difficult by stages but the responses required of the child remain fairly simple. The language of this unit is organized around six themes, i.e. *position, what does it mean, what happens if, comparison, the reason why* and *time*. The materials also include pre-recorded cassettes, a specimen workbook, prompt answer cards and spirit duplicator masters.

Unit Two deals with concept building with the express aim of increasing children's skill and flexibility in classifying data. Central to Unit Two is the idea of the matrix (Fig. 4.1) which helps children to sort objects into sets.

The Matrix sheets are grids of pictures arranged in columns and rows according to the classes to which the items featured in the pictures belong. The essential data on each new Matrix is introduced to the class and this is reinforced by individual or group activities. In addition there is a series of workcards with each Matrix to provide experience in writing. The materials in Unit Two also include activity books, magnet cards, small Matrix cards, Matrix builders and missing picture books.

Unit Three aims to increase the children's oral skills of description and enquiry. In this unit the pupils work in groups and practise their skills of description with each other. The materials contain sheets of pictures of monsters (Fig. 4.2 below).

c

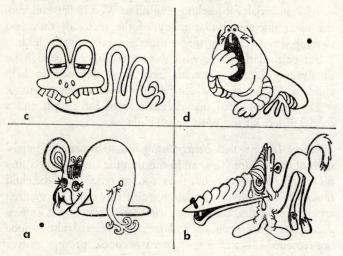

Fig. 4.2 *Picture sheets from Unit 3 of* CONCEPT 7-11.

The children have to describe each monster in sufficient detail for the other children to identify it. As the children progress the pictures become more difficult to describe. In addition this unit contains materials for children working in pairs with a screen between them. One has a Symbol Drawing Book with a simple design; he describes this design to the child on the other side of the screen, who makes a drawing of the original design. The picture is then returned to the first child who can judge the effectiveness of his description. Other materials in this unit which increase skill in asking questions include a detective enquiry game and a treasure hunt game.

The Dialect Kit is to assist the teacher working with children of Caribbean origin who have dialect difficulties in writing standard English. The kit contains a short test to identify those children who need to use the dialect kit (see extract below, Fig. 4.3). The general pattern of use of the kit is short, teacher-led sessions with a group of children, reinforced by individual work by the children.

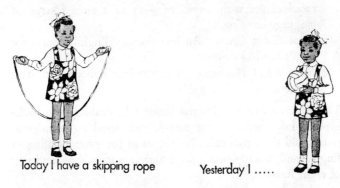

Today I have a skipping rope   Yesterday I .....

Fig. 4.3 *Illustration from the Dialect kit,* CONCEPT 7–11.

The kit also contains a 'Right for Writing' book, flash cards, sentence cards and a magnet card. There is also a comprehensive teachers' manual for each unit and one for the dialect kit. Each unit contains sufficient quantities of material to enable both large and small groups to work with it.

Asian pupils and the SCOPE materials

These materials,[2] based upon the Schools Council Project in English for Immigrant Children established at Leeds University, were produced because experience had indicated that there were large numbers of non-English speaking immigrant children (mainly of Asian origin) in British Schools, who would benefit from the production of a specially tailored language kit. Of equal importance was the fact that teachers were in need of practical help, especially in the teaching of English to those pupils:

The materials were developed in four main areas:

1 *Scope Stage 1* An introductory English course for non-English speaking pupils of 8–13.
2 *Scope Stage 2* A language development course for multiracial classes with pupils of 8–13 at a second stage of language learning.
3 *Scope Senior Course* An introductory English course for pupils aged 14 or over.
4 *Scope Infant Handbook* A curriculum bulletin for infant teachers.

There are also two additional handbooks dealing with background information about non-English speaking immigrant pupils and their particular difficulties in the pronunciation of English and, to supplement *Scope Stage 1*, a storybook, and a set of eight Readers.

Scope Stage 1: An introductory English course for immigrant children

This course is intended for use in British schools with non-English-Speaking children between the age of 8–13, although it can be adapted for use with younger and older pupils.

AIMS OF THE COURSE

Throughout the course the aim is to help teachers give their pupils a sound elementary knowledge of spoken English and then to start them reading and writing English. Most teachers of minority ethnic group pupils have had little or no experience of teaching English as a second language and the course is deliberately designed to help them learn the techniques of this kind of teaching and to see that their pupils learn the language as thoroughly and economically as possible.

For many non-English-speaking children there is the added difficulty of trying to settle down to an entirely new way of life. The material provided with the course and topics selected for the language scheme are designed to help the children become familiar with everyday aspects of English life which are strange to them.

ARRANGEMENT OF THE COURSE

This course is centred around fourteen topics. Both in the oral scheme and in the reading and writing material reference is made to a group of children and their families, all of different nationalities, who live in King Street. These topics and the theme of the King Street children and their families are the focus of interest for the language scheme and the Readers. The topics have been selected to give the children the opportunity to learn the vocabulary and structures which they will need to use in everyday situations: some of them also introduce the language of simple subject teaching.

The topics of the fourteen units are as follows: The classroom, King Street: Shopping: Clothes: Family and home: The park: Stories: Seeing the doctor: The fire: An island: Animals: Farm animals and farming: The post office: The railway station.

THE VISUAL MATERIAL

Immigrant children have to cope with many new concepts and experiences when settling into school in Britain. The language necessary to deal with these has to be learnt in as tangible a way as possible. In addition to talking about actual objects, the children need to get used to recognizing pictures of them. The cut-out figures used with the simple background pictures have been designed to enable the teacher and pupil to build up a variety of complete visual aids to suit their needs.

THE LANGUAGE SCHEME

This is contained in the Teacher's Book and is the basis of the whole course. Emphasis throughout is laid on the structural patterns of English: the pupils will tend to learn vocabulary fairly easily, but their main need is to learn the way in which words are put together and the correct forms of those words. The Teacher's Book also contains 'Story' and 'Reading and Writing' sections which are directly linked with the oral language scheme.

LENGTH OF THE COURSE AND FLEXIBILITY OF MATERIALS

Most children will need at least two terms to master the language in the course. Situations and the time available for teaching English to non-English-speaking children vary widely from area to area and it is recognized that teachers must as far as possible be able to work through the course at their own pace. One of the main features of the course, therefore, is its flexibility for use in a variety of teaching situations.

Scope Stage 2: A language development course

This is a language development course designed for use in British schools with children of 8–13. The materials are intended for use in multiracial classes in which children need special help with the development of language skills, whether they are learners of English as a second language, children who speak a dialect of English, or other native speakers who apparently have difficulty in their use of English at school. The materials aim to assist teachers to develop through the medium of normal class teaching, their pupils' use of English as a tool for learning, thinking and communicating.

AIMS OF THE COURSE

Teachers of classes such as those described above may very often have had no specialist training in language teaching. The materials therefore aim to give teachers:

1 An awareness of the nature of language.
2 Guidance in language-teaching techniques in the context of general class teaching.

3. Help with class organization where levels of ability and language development vary considerably.

LANGUAGE DEVELOPMENT

The materials are based on three themes, Homes, Travel and Water. The language learning content relates to the demands of the themes, as does the reading and writing material.

The thematic approach, with content and concept as important as language practice and incorporating a systematic approach to oral and written language, should help to counter (a) the low motivation which may result from learning language for the sake of language and (b) the demoralization which sets in from continual failure in educational skills.

As the scheme for language development is taken from the demands of each theme it does not follow the more usual step-by-step grading of a language course but gives opportunities throughout for children to use language they already know, and to learn and practise new language in contexts which are relevant both to their needs and to their interests.

THE MATERIALS

The Pupils' Books (see Fig. 4.5):
Homes, Travel and *Water* each contain information, stories, poems and a large number of pictures and photographs, and are intended as the common starting point for the children's work on a theme. Each is divided into a series of topics, called sections.

A selection of section headings:

Homes. Buildings; What are buildings made of? Building a house; At home; Animals and their homes; Homes in different areas of the world.

Travel. Local travel; Travelling for work; Animals that migrate; Emigrating; Forced to move; Space travel.

Water. At sea; Fish and fishing; Fresh water life; Sinking and floating; Too much water; Not enough water.

The Teacher's Book

This book, the core of the scheme, provides a commentary on the function and structure of the language in the Pupils' Books and suggests, in a series of activities for each of the sections, ways in which topics can be introduced and expanded (see above). At the same time, these activities provide opportunities for practising and developing language in use. The last activity in each section is normally a workshop in which

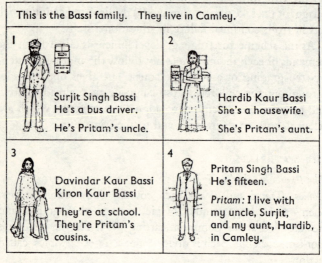

This is the Bassi family.   They live in Camley.

1   Surjit Singh Bassi
He's a bus driver.
He's Pritam's uncle.

2   Hardib Kaur Bassi
She's a housewife.
She's Pritam's aunt.

3   Davindar Kaur Bassi
Kiron Kaur Bassi
They're at school.
They're Pritam's cousins.

4   Pritam Singh Bassi
He's fifteen.
Pritam: I live with my uncle, Surjit, and my aunt, Hardib, in Camley.

Fig. 4.4 *From Scope Senior Course, Student's Book One,* We Live in England.

children and teacher participate, and which gives an opportunity for the class as a whole to consolidate the work done.

The work cards

The cards are an essential part of the course's approach; they enable the children to engage in extensive individual or group study appropriate to their needs and at the same time to get considerable practice in the various language skills. The cards

Look at the pictures in each group.
Who does these things in your home?
Use this sentence to help you.
    My mother does the *cooking*.

Have you got any jobs at home?
What are they?
Do you do them every day?
Do you do them every week?

Which jobs do you never do?
Which jobs do you always do?
Which jobs do you sometimes do?

Ask your friend some questions.

Think of some other jobs.

Fig. 4.5 *From Scope Stage Two, Pupil's Book,* Homes.

are written at three different levels of difficulty to cater for a broad range of ability within the class. Since these cannot, however, provide for the needs and interests of every class, the teacher is encouraged to write many more of his own. The complete set of work cards contains 54 double-sided cards, colour coded to denote the level of difficulty.

Scope Senior Course

Scope Senior Course is primarily intended for recently arrived non-English speaking students aged 14 or over, but can also be used with adult beginners.

AIMS OF THE COURSE

The immediate aim of the course is to give the students a sound elementary knowledge of spoken English and to help them to read and write it. The wider aim is to prepare students for adult life among native English speakers. The language of the course has been carefully structured so that the students progress from simple and controlled language related to the immediate environment in Book 1, through more complex situations and language in Book 2, to the language of interviews and business letters in Book 3. Another important aim is to cater for the very wide range of ability and educational background of students who may be following the course.

Scope Handbooks 1 and 2 are recommended as reference books for teachers using the course. The course falls into two main parts, the first covered by Books 1 and 2, and the second by Book 3.

THE MATERIALS

Students' Book One (see Fig. 4.5)
We live in England is set in the imaginary town of Camley, and deals with day-to-day activities that may be unfamiliar to newly arrived immigrants. For example: Names and address: Can you tell me the way? Can you mend this? At the grocer's; You're late; The launderette.

The tape
The tape, Radio Camley, is based on the style of a local radio

station, and consolidates the language learned in Book 1 through the popular appeal of jingles, bulletins, interviews, etc. The presentation and content of Radio Camley are an innovation in language-teaching materials, and the tape has particular value as aural comprehension material.

Student's Book Two
Out and about in England goes further afield in subject matter to such topics as: the evening institute; towns and villages in England; the post office; travel arrangements; the emergency services; pollution.

Wall pictures
There are six large wall pictures to accompany the Students' Books for class language practice.

The Teacher's Book
This is an essential guide to the use of the two Students' Books. It provides advice on how to present the materials to students of different ability and educational background and includes four chapters on teaching method, which form a useful guide for teachers new to the methodology of language teaching: Listening and speaking; The tape recorder; Reading and writing; Language games. There is an appendix entitled; A grammatical description of some of the language in this course.

(Also recommended for use with illiterate students are the Picture Cards, Picture Book, Work Book, Work Cards, Word Slips and Readers from Scope Stage 1.)

Students' Book Three: Ready For Work
This part of the course aims to instruct students who have a sound knowledge of basic English in developing and using the practical knowledge involved in leaving school and gaining employment. Although of greatest value for use with multi-racial leaving classes and newly-arrived immigrant adults, the skills imparted by the materials would also prove most

useful for students who wish to pursue their studies further, whether full-time or at evening classes. 'Ready for work' provides a scheme of study centred on topics of interest to students in the situations described above. It contains sections dealing with such subjects as: preparing for interviews; filling in application forms; telephoning for appointments; writing letters; attending interviews.

Each section contains dialogues, exercises, photographs, cartoons, specimen forms, questionnaires, etc., to stimulate initial questions and discussion from which further language work will develop, and to encourage self-assessment and criticism.

Work book
This provides extra opportunity for practice in writing letters, filling in forms, etc.

The tape
This contains many of the dialogues and some of the exercises in the Student's Book, and drills.

The Teacher's Book
This is essential for the effective use of the materials. It contains teaching notes on the presentation of the materials, the tape-script, and appendices concerned with language skills particularly relevant to this part of the course, and with background knowledge needed by the teacher of a class of school leavers.

Scope storybook

A collection of illustrated stories for the teacher to read to pupils in multiracial classes in primary schools. The subject matter and language of some of the stories link with the language scheme of Scope Stage 1, and the stories are grouped according to approximate linguistic grading. The accompanying Teacher's Notes suggest ways in which the language of the stories can be practised through games, songs and other activities.

Scope supplementary readers – plays and dialogues

Eight illustrated readers designed to supplement the Scope Stage 1 series of readers. The eight books are written at the level of the later Stage 1 readers. Each book contains short Teachers' Notes at the end. Most of the plays and dialogues are very short, and are centred on the activities, both in and out of school, of the King Street children and other characters well known to users of Stage 1. The books also contain some folk tales.

Scope handbooks

Handbook 1: The social background of immigrant children from India, Pakistan and Cyprus
A handbook on the cultural backgrounds of immigrants from India, Pakistan and Cyprus of use to teachers of the children of immigrants as well as of adults and children who are themselves immigrants.

Handbook 2: Pronunciation: for immigrant children from India, Pakistan, Cyprus and Italy
The pronunciation of English is a special problem for all learners of English as a second language. The handbook is particularly useful for teachers who have not had any specific training in language teaching. Part 1 deals with the major features of pronunciations which have to be taught and the techniques of how to teach them. Part 2 deals with the main difficulties experienced by speakers of other languages, grouping these accordingly and giving detailed practice material to help.

Other language materials

In addition the journal *Multi-Racial School* (formerly *English for Immigrants*) includes articles by practising teachers giving useful suggestions on particular teaching problems and on the use of teaching aids. Many publishers produce catalogues of materials specifically designed for the teaching of English as a second language, (e.g. Longmans, *Ways to English for the multiracial classroom*.) Apart from the major schemes already discussed there are a number of others that practising teachers have found useful and although this list is not exhaustive some of these are briefly described here.

1.   *Situational English* (Published by the Longman Group Ltd)
This well established course for adult students of English was originally adapted from a course prepared for non-English speaking immigrants to Australia. It has since proved very successful in teaching adult non-English speakers in Britain and as such is comparable to the Scope Senior Course. The approach used is aural–oral based on the situational method and the 'Language Picture Series' provides the teacher with additional situations. In addition there is a very useful Teachers' Book with detailed suggestions and advice on the teaching of each unit.

2.   *SRA Language Development Programme* (Published by Science Research Associates)
The Programme contains 96 Language Builder storyboards that provide material for discussion. These boards are deliberately open-ended to encourage a variety of interpretations, and to let children demonstrate in language their grasp of concepts being presented.

Through group discussion, the children develop their own story and dialogue according to their particular language needs. An unusually detailed Teachers' Guidebook provides every spur to conversation the teacher needs to help them do this, and much more.

When the group agrees on a dialogue, the teacher may write it on special papers and stick it to the panel. As well as helping develop a story, the children benefit from seeing that written language records their own words. This serves as an excellent visual instruction to the function of reading. The Programme aims not only at improving the child's spoken language, but also at increasing his conceptual abilities. Using the boards, he can see each panel as part of a whole story. He is encouraged to remember sequence in order to summarize the story. In talking about familiar home and community situations, he sees how his actions affect others and how their's affect him. Science Research Associates recommend Language Development as a flexible programme for all kinds of children at many levels of education: 'Any child can benefit . . . little ones who are still developing language patterns . . . *children who don't speak English* and need an introduction to community life in a different country'. The Language Development Programme has been found to be suited to the integrated day and individualized programmes. Children can work in pairs, progressing at their own rate, and it's equally effective when used in groups.

3. *Absorbing English* (Published by the Longman Group Ltd) Originally designed for pupils overseas this course is suitable for non-English speaking pupils between the ages of 8–10 years. The course is based on the activity group work method and provides a solid foundation of elementary grammar building up a vocabulary of about 1,000 words. Also the workbooks provide additional written practice for children already familiar with Roman script.

4. *Hello-Hello series*
'Hello-Hello' is a series of 10 tapes from the original BBC series previously broadcast and edited in consultation with the Schools Council Project in English for Immigrant Children. All the tapes are graded and each one uses language up to an approximate unit of the Scope Stage I course. Although the tapes are intended for non-English speaking children between the ages of 8–11 they have been used with other children experiencing linguistic difficulties. Each programme is presented in a lively manner and lasts between $8\frac{1}{2}$ and $9\frac{1}{2}$ minutes. The topics will

be enjoyed by junior age children and the stories, which are drawn from various cultures include such titles as 'Guru Nanak and Mardana'; 'Ananse and the Jar of Bees' and 'Kuldip's Dream'.

Second-stage immigrant learners

How do immigrant children fare once they have left the language or reception centre and take their place in an ordinary school? This is the question dealt with in *The Continuing Needs of Immigrants*, the survey published by the Department of Education and Science in 1972.[3]

During the school year 1969/1970 a group of HM Inspectors carried out a survey in 54 secondary schools in 16 areas. The survey deals with the 'high number of immigrant pupils who have overcome the initial difficulties of communication and need to go forward towards a gradual mastery of more demanding and complex language'. Various arrangements are made for the reception of immigrant pupils. In only 6 of the 16 areas surveyed were there reception and English language teaching centres. One of these centres took all such secondary age children arriving from overseas and kept them for 4–8 weeks. During this time the centre aimed at equipping pupils with enough spoken English to cope with the work of a normal school curriculum. The survey points out that 'for those who come with no knowledge of the English language to do this during a maximum of eight weeks hardly seems feasible'.

In some areas with no centres the local education authorities are assisting the schools with the provision of extra help and support in the form of staff and equipment. But the survey points out that 'in one or two areas no reception arrangements of any kind exist for immigrant pupils of secondary school age and they simply turn up at school and are admitted without anything being known about their background. Too often such pupils are admitted into normal remedial classes and do not receive the special help that they need.'

In contrast, one area operating an induction centre 'recognizes the need for continuing support to former full-time immigrant pupils by arranging for centre staff to visit secondary schools and keep in touch with them for up to 9 months after they have left the centre'.

The survey also considered the procedures used where pupils were transferred from special classes or centres to the ordinary school or class. The Inspectors found that most centres tested the pupil in various skills before deciding to put him back into the normal school environment.

In some schools they found that the decision to move a pupil from a special class was determined by the arrival of new pupils creating a pressure on special class places. There was, they say, 'occasionally clear evidence that some intelligent immigrant pupils, who would have benefited from a longer intensive English language teaching course, had been moved into the main stream of school organization at remedial class or lower stream level, to their educational disadvantage'.

More attention must be given, says the survey, to the transfer from special to normal classes. English Departments should become involved in the decision-making. Both oral and written language needs to be taken into account. However, 'it must be emphasized that when pupils return to a normal class they will nearly always require continuing help with language, and subject specialists need to consider how far this may involve a modified approach in the classroom'.

The survey examined the policies of the 16 local education authorities involved in the study and concluded that 'only one of the local education authorities covered by the survey has clearly accepted the need for special second-phase provision at the secondary level and has consciously evolved an official policy in this field'. Within the schools themselves a variety of arrangements exists. The survey found that many members of staff knew little about the work of the language and reception centres and rarely sought the advice of the centres on materials or methods. Many of the schools visited made no special arrangements for the minority ethnic group pupils admitted from junior schools. In streamed secondary schools pupils were usually placed in lower streams thus presenting the teacher of such classes with both slow-learning indigenous children and minority ethnic group children of mixed ability.

The Inspectors found that in many schools 'once the pupils have transferred into normal classes they may be left very much on their own from the language point of view'. Language difficulties hamper able immigrant pupils throughout their education career, the survey instances one group of sixth-form science pupils who were dispirited at the state of their English and their inability to pass 'O' level English.

The special needs of minority ethnic group pupils are regarded by many subject teachers as being outside their responsibility. The survey reports that 'few members of staff, other than specialist language staff, were found to have attended appropriate courses or to have read any background material about immigrant pupils'. English Departments did not possess much knowledge or experience in the teaching of English as a second language and 'liaison between the English department and the specialist language classes was rarely found to be well developed'.

The survey also found little evidence of modifications of the curriculum to adapt to the changed population of the school. In teaching English through literature the texts used could be reconsidered in the light of linguistic difficulty and subject matter. As the report says, books with an Asian and Caribbean background, stories and myths, books of general knowledge are liked by many minority ethnic group pupils. Elementary background knowledge about pupils from overseas can be a great help to a subject teacher. 'Such knowledge', the report goes on, 'enables the useful but casual illusion to be made that demonstrates the teachers' interest in the individual . . . geographical, historical, religious knowledge of the pupils' country of origin is generally stimulating to teachers, reminding them frequently that their own traditional subject matter may be becoming out of touch with a changing world'.

The report concludes by pointing out that more 'positive thinking and constructive action' is needed in educating second-phase immigrant pupils. Language is the basis of the difficulties of these children, and also of many socially and culturally disadvantaged indigenous children. 'All teachers and would-be teachers would profit from opportunities to study the structure of the English language and how it works'. Many minority ethnic group pupils have difficulty in finding employment on leaving school. 'It is possible', says the report, 'that their difficulties would be less serious if they received more consistent informed help during their second-phase education in the secondary school.'

Summary

It is apparent that the teaching of English to non-English-speaking pupils is seen by multiracial schools as their major task. Schools deal with this problem in many different ways according to their own philosophy and to the resources made available by local education authorities. What is not so clear is the level of proficiency in English at which schools decide that no further special arrangements are necessary. The tests of proficiency in English developed by the National Foundation for Educational Research may assist schools in devising their own criteria for judging the proficiency in English, for it seems that many schools end their special arrangements at too early a stage, when competence has been achieved at a conversational level but not at a sufficiently high level to enable future success in secondary education. The question of 'second stage' English following the initial achievement of literacy appears as yet to be imperfectly understood in either the need or the approach. There is often little feedback of information between reception centres and their respective secondary schools resulting in the efforts of the former being somewhat negated when the pupils move on. Obviously some kind of informal induction of immigrant pupils into the receiving secondary schools should be initiated if 'second stage' English is to be achieved together with wider integration into the school society. In this respect the evidence of the Community Relations Commission to the Committee of Inquiry into Reading and the use of English is a particularly illuminating and interesting summary of many of the linguistic problems that confront pupils from minority ethnic groups based upon research studies undertaken over a number of years.

This book is primarily concerned with minority ethnic groups from India, Pakistan, Bangladesh and the West Indies. However, in certain cities, e.g. Liverpool, Chinese pupils form a large proportion of the children who have to learn English as a second language. I have therefore decided to include a brief section on some of the English Language difficulties that confront this particular minority group.

Some English language difficulties for Chinese speakers

INTRODUCTION

The majority of Chinese people in Britain come from Hong Kong and speak Cantonese, a dialect of Chinese quite distinct from Mandarin, the Chinese National Language. Spoken Cantonese and Mandarin are mutually unintelligible, although the written language is virtually the same. (See THE WRITTEN LANGUAGE *below*.)

PRONUNCIATION DIFFICULTIES

Cantonese lacks a number of the consonants used in English. The Cantonese speaker tends to identify English sounds with the sounds he knows, and so confuses many English sounds, e.g.

f and *v* (lea*f* and lea*v*e), since Cantonese has no v.

s, z, sh and '*ʒ*' – the voiced sound in mea*s*ure (*s*ort and *sh*ort, *s*aid and *z*ed, Confu*ci*an and confu*s*ion), since Cantonese has only *s* and *sy*.

f and unvoiced *th* (*f*ree and *th*ree); *d* and voiced *th* (*d*en and *th*en) – Cantonese has no *th* sounds.

ch and *j* (*ch*eap and *j*eep).

p and *b, t* and *d, k* and *g*, especially when they occur between vowels (pe*ck*ing and pe*gg*ing) and at the end of words (ni*p* and ni*b*, no*t* and no*d*, do*ck* and do*g*).

Cantonese has no *b, d, g*; at the beginning of words it uses either unaspirated *p, t, k* which sound rather like our *b, d, g*; or aspirated *p, t, k* which are similar to our *p, t, k*. At the end of words *p, t* and *k* are not 'exploded' and so are hardly audible.

l, n and *r* (*l*ice, *n*ice and *r*ice): in Cantonese *l* is frequently substituted for *n*, so the Cantonese speaker may even confuse words like leg and neck!

Final *l* may be replaced by *w* -bi*ll*, we*ll*). Together with the clipped final consonants *p, t, k*, etc. this may produce something of a Cockney effect.

The Cantonese speaker does not have the same difficulties with vowels, except for the difference between long and short vowels (d*o*ck and d*a*rk, l*i*d and l*ea*d); he finds it very difficult to distinguish fift*een* and fif*ty*.

Cantonese words are all monosyllables or combinations of monosyllables, and of a simple type: either consonant-vowel-consonant (e.g. yat, sap) or consonant-vowel/diphthong (e.g. yi, sei). There is therefore only a small range of possible words, but they are distinguished by tones. There are no clusters of consonants as in *st*reet, *spr*ing, li*fts*, twe*lfths*, so such words must be taught very carefully.

Only very few consonants are possible at the end of Cantonese words (*m*, *n*, *ng* and the barely audible *p*, *t* and *k*). This explains why Cantonese speakers have great difficulty in hearing and reproducing final consonants. They may even say something like 'Ye' i' i' ' for 'Yes it is'.

GRAMMAR

Cantonese has the following significant features:

(*a*) There are no inflexions or word changes to denote plurals, tenses, comparatives, subject, object, gender, etc. The word ngóh means I and me; the word kéuih means he, him, she, her and it. There are suffixes which can be added to words to denote past time, but they are not used if the tense is obvious from the context.

(*b*) Cantonese frequently does not use an equivalent of (i) the articles 'a' and 'the'; (ii) the verbs 'is' and 'are', the conjunction 'and', the preposition 'to'. 'In', 'on', 'at' and 'from' are expressed by the same preposition.

(*c*) Nouns and adjectives, e.g. China and Chinese, have the same form.

Cantonese sentences sound rather like telegram English when translated, e.g.

Ngóh máaih syù=I buy book=I buy

I am buying	a book
I shall buy	some books
I bought	the book
I have bought	the books
I had bought	

Jùnggwok★ syù gwai★ ma?=China book expensive, eh?
=Are Chinese books expensive?

★ 'g' in these words represents the unaspirated 'k'.

It is easy to understand how the Cantonese speaker produces pidgin English such as the following:

Yesterday I go shop buy ice-cream.

THE WRITTEN LANGUAGE

Written Chinese uses several thousand distinct characters, each representing an idea or meaning, not a set of sounds. In this way the same written form can be used for different dialects, such as Mandarin and Cantonese. Chinese characters can be compared with mathematical symbols or numerals, which are internationally recognized but read differently by speakers of different languages.

Chinese education has traditionally laid great emphasis on calligraphy and the memorization of the written characters. Chinese pupils transfer these skills to English, learning to copy neatly and memorizing the spelling of whole words: common faults however are copying without understanding and failure to see links between sound and spelling.

SOME FURTHER DIFFICULTIES: NAMES, RELATIONS AND AGES

Misunderstanding can easily arise when the teacher tries to obtain from his pupil (*a*) his surname, (*b*) the number of brothers and sisters and (*c*) his age.

(*a*) *Names.* The Chinese custom is to put the surname first. Next come either one or two 'given names' or personal names. In many cases where a person has two given names he shares the first of these with other brothers and sisters. However Chinese children take readily to the idea of an English Christian name for use in school.

We had two brothers called Wong Chi Dock and Wong Chi Moon. Wong was their surname and Chi a name which they shared. To conform with English usage they soon began to put their surname last, becoming Chi Dock Wong and Chi

Moon Wong. They were then given English Christian names and became known as Tony Wong and Robert Wong.

(b) The question 'How many brothers have you?' may produce the reply 'Two brothers' when the teacher knows that the pupil has only one brother. The pupil is in fact thinking in terms of 'How many brothers are there?' since Cantonese uses the same word for 'have' and 'there are'.

(c) *Ages*. Chinese pupils often give their age as one year older, or possibly two years older, than the teacher expects. According to Chinese tradition a child is one year old at birth (the nine months in the womb) and becomes two years old at the next Chinese New Year.

USEFUL BOOKS

Teach Yourself Cantonese (English Universities Press), for the spoken language.

Teach Yourself Chinese (English Universities Press), for Mandarin and the written language.

Better English Pronunciation, J. D. O'Connor (Cambridge University Press, 1967). The appendix on difficulties of English pronunciation for speakers of Cantonese, Arabic, Hindi, etc. is particularly useful.

About Chinese, Richard Newnham and Tan Lim-Tung (Penguin Books, 1971)

Speak Cantonese, Parker Huang (Far Eastern Publications, Yale University Press). Obtainable from Collet's Chinese Bookshop, Great Russell Street, London WC1.

Chinese in London, Ng Kwee Choo (Oxford University Press for the Institute of Race Relations, 1968)

There was a study of Chinese children in Britain financed by the Social Science Research Council and the Noel Buton Trust, which recommended that the DES (possibly through the Schools Council) should set up a working party of teachers to work out professional guidelines and materials for colleagues who have small groups of Chinese children in their classes. They also recommended that holiday schools should be made available to Chinese children as to other immigrant pupils. Local authorities organize or encourage Saturday morning schools, evening groups or holiday learning schemes for West Indian, Pakistani, Bengali, or Indian children. Excellent though these are, they seldom attract or hold many Chinese children because of their different needs, outlook and behaviour. Clearly special provision of this kind needs to be made by local authorities for Chinese children under the various programmes especially those sponsored by the Home Office.

And, finally, we obviously need more research. During the course of their study the authors were astounded by the lack of knowledge about and the amount of prejudice towards Chinese children.

Books for multiracial schools

A related issue to the language difficulties experienced by pupils who belong to minority ethnic groups is often the lack of a reading scheme which reflects the multiracial classroom. All too often, the reading schemes available feature an all-white environment far from the experience of inner city children. As an example of a scheme which attempts to redress the balance the SPARKS scheme is described in detail.

SPARKS: *An Infant Reading Scheme for Children in an Urban Environment*,[4] is an attempt to give the teacher a reading scheme which reflects the background of inner city children. The scheme also tries to give the children some of the pre-reading experience they might not have received at home and to awaken their curiosity and interest in books. The books reflect a world of streets and flats, supermarkets and bingo, fish and chips. The authors have tried to move away from the dull descriptive prose of many reading schemes and the majority of the books in the SPARKS scheme tell a complete and meaningful story. Some of the books are shaped in an unusual way or have pockets attached for sentence matching cards. The scheme is divided into six stages and the practical suggestions given in the teacher's book for further activities at each stage are an essential part of the whole scheme.

Stage One covers the pre-reading stage in the child's development and consists of 12 pre-readers, a Teacher's Storybook and a concertina book. The pre-readers, on subjects such as Drains, Puddles, My Zip, My Injection, My Jeans, My Ladybird, Something in My Eye, provide a simple story that is easily remembered and a situation which every child can recognize. They are rhythmic and partly repetitive. It is suggested that the teacher can read these books with individual children or in a group and then place them in the book corner for children to use themselves. The aim is for the children to read the short stories without the need to identify every word. At this stage also there are eight teacher's storybooks about the Sparks family which the teacher can read to the children.

The teacher's book gives other ideas for pre-reading activities such as 'making children's name cards and devising games with them, making homemade books about outings, models, pets, cooking or other individual interests.' A list of books to supplement Stage One is also given.

Stage Two consists of Family Booklets with accompanying sentence matching cards and Family Shaped books with matching work cards. The Family Booklets have pockets turned up on the outside to hold the matching cards. There are four Family Shaped books: *The Flats, Mum and the Supermarket, Dad and his Lorry, Gran and Grandad.* The main aim of this stage is to help develop sight vocabulary and this is the purpose of the sets of matching cards. Practical suggestions at this stage include, 'the teacher can play a game with the matching word cards, usually with only four or five children at a time. After distributing the small cards for a particular shaped book to the children so that they each have five or six in front of them, she then holds up a large card and says, 'Who has this word, "lorry"?' The child matches this against his own cards and claims it if appropriate. Other suggestions are 'As a follow-up to this children can make books about their own families, using the cards from the booklets, and make additional cards to construct sentences about themselves', or 'Scrap books using pictures cut from magazines or advertisements and models can be made about supermarkets, cars and lorries, flats and houses.'

Stage Three concentrates on the immediate environment, going to the park, to the cinema, to a football match. It contains eight booklets, eight larger books and a picture alphabet folder. When all the books in this stage have been read all the more common consonants will have been covered.

Stage Four gives practice in phonic skills. It provides books on two topics: the weather and school. The school books contain a more advanced vocabulary than the weather books. The suggestion is made that some work on auditory discrimination of vowels should be introduced about halfway through this stage and the practical ideas in the teacher's book give various vowel card games which emphasize the children listening to the sounds before matching them to the appropriate written form.

Stage Five consists of four longer books on Festivals and Holidays. Practical suggestions for this stage include ideas for practising phonic skills, such as the phonic wheel illustrated below.

Stage Six consists of eight Funny and Exciting Books on subjects such as the Man from Mars, Witches and Wishes, Monsters and Ghosts, Charlie the Chimp. The books are all illustrated in full colour with limp laminated covers, except for the teacher's story book which has a stiff cover.

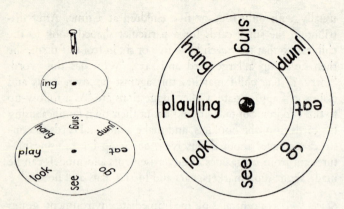

Fig. 4.6 *An illustration from* SPARKS, Teacher's Book.

Choice of reading material

The present writer[5] in an investigation involving West Indian and indigenous adolescents found that the former group rejected their own colour. I commented at the time that this was probably because throughout their history they have always been orientated towards England. The English 'model' and ways can still play an important part in West Indian psychology and this can lead to a rejection of all that is West Indian. Such rejection has in the past, been enhanced by the use in West Indian schools of books and other materials which emphasize the 'white image', portraying white heroes, white angels, a white god and generally glorify a light coloured skin. A dark skin is deemed to be of inferior status. Such self-rejection can produce feelings of inferiority, which in turn can affect attitudes and behaviour. Obviously one of the many ways in which West Indian and other minority ethnic group children can be assisted in their creation of an acceptable self-image, which is so important to the development of a harmonious multiracial society, is in the choice of reading and other illustrative material.

In this respect there have been a number of surveys of children's books which have examined the contents and assessed how this may affect the child's view of other groups in the community. Two such ventures are:

Books for Children: The Homelands of Immigrants in Britain, edited by Janet Hill, Institute of Race Relations.
Sowing the Dragons Teeth – racial bias in the books we teach, – Liverpool Community Relations Commission.

For children growing up in a multiracial society books can play a vital part in the development of awareness and understanding. They have the power to involve children of different backgrounds, cultures and religions: and, as previously intimated, the power to give the child a sense of pride in his own cultural heritage. A considerable amount of literature is now available which take account of the points I have been emphasizing. Three booklists that can be instantly recommended, although there are undoubtedly more, are:

A Bibliography for Teachers, Community Relations Commission.
Books for the Multi-Racial Classroom, compiled by Janet Elkin, published by the National Book League.
The Library in the Multi-Racial Secondary School: A Caribbean Book List by Alison Day. (Available from the Community Relations Commission.)

Unfortunately in the past many of the books depicting minority ethnic group children (especially older pupils) in a multiracial society have tended to over-emphasize the problems and conflicts that might occur. In such a situation the children will find difficulty in identifying themselves as normal and acceptable members of the community. One hopes that in the future books will be written which take the multiracial society for granted and in which the central themes are ordinary adventures and excitements.

References

1 National Book League (1973) *English for Immigrant Children.* An annotated list.

2 SCOPE *An Introductory English Course for Immigrant Children.* Schools Council/Longman.

3 *The Continuing Needs of Immigrants*, Education Survey 14. DES/HMSO, 1972.

4 SPARKS: *An Infant Reading Scheme for Children in an Urban Environment.* Blackie & Son.

5 Hill, D. (1970) The attitudes of West Indian and English adolescents in Britain. *Race* 11, 3.

6 Day, A. (1971) The library in the multiracial school: a Caribbean book list. *School Librarian* (the journal of the School Library Association) **19,** 3, September.

7 Garvey, A. & Jackson, B. (1974) *Chinese Children.* Cambridge Educational Development Trust.

5

Other aspects of the teacher's task

Introduction

The lesson to be learnt from this chapter is perhaps the extent to which the vast majority of multiracial schools have adapted to new circumstances and the majority of pupils and parents have accepted the demands of a new and completely different environment.

None of the 'problem areas' that are mentioned affect the majority of schools and in this respect the word 'problem' may be a misnomer. The point really being stressed in this section is that here are some sources of possible culture conflict with which the teacher *may* have to deal. Forewarned is forearmed, and it is towards developing in teachers a sensitivity towards and a fuller understanding of these possibly difficult areas that this section is directed.

Past research into what are considered to be the most frequently reported problems in multiracial schools would seem to indicate that both schools and parents need to know a lot more about each other's way of life. Even when the knowledge exists it is not always acted upon. For example, school meals can be a source of difficulty because part of the common English menus are often not acceptable to some minority ethnic groups. The area of discipline is one which is reported frequently, particularly when the schools in question contain a fair proportion of West Indian pupils. However, in this respect there are a number of important factors. First there is the fact that many teachers have stereotyped the West Indian pupil as ill-behaved, and second is the Caribbean-based expectation of his parents that discipline and control in an English school will be repressive.

One should never, of course, make generalizations about the characteristics or customs of any ethnic group. For example, many differences occur in the life styles of Asians between Moslems and Hindus, the former being in general much more conservative. After puberty a Hindu girl can wear a sari and earrings, and is conscious about beautifying and displaying herself within the existing framework of the cultural background. On the other hand a Moslem girl of the same age would tend to be covering up more of her body.

It seems therefore, that a greater involvement of parents in the life of schools and greater knowledge among teachers of the background and expectations of immigrant parents would offer a start to finding ways of coping with differences. However, such topics as food, dress, co-education etc. are not important in themselves. What is important is to encourage a more open attitude of mind, and once this is done the adjustments in these and similar areas will be made by the individuals themselves.

Religious education

Section 25 of the 1944 Education Act specifies important provisions relating to religious education in schools. The provisions most relevant to this chapter are found in paragraphs one, two and four of the Section which are quoted below. As it can be very misleading to isolate statements from a document such as this Act, the reader is recommended to consult the full text for details of the many provisions relating to these paragraphs.

1 Subject to the provisions of this section, the school day in every county school and in every voluntary school shall begin with collective worship on the part of all pupils in attendance at the school, and the arrangements made therefore shall provide for a single act of worship attended by all such pupils unless, in the opinion of the local education authority or, in the case of a voluntary school, of the managers or governors thereof, the school premises are such as to make it impracticable to assemble them for that purpose.

2 Subject to the provisions of this section, religious instruction shall be given in every county school and in every voluntary school.

4 If the parent of any pupil in attendance at any county school or any voluntary school requests that he be wholly or partly excused from attendance at religious worship in the school, or from attendance at religious instruction in the school, or from attendance at both religious worship and religious instruction in the school, then, until the request is withdrawn, the pupil shall be excused from such attendance accordingly.

In the conditions prevailing in 1944 the changing population of our schools was not foreseen and nowhere in the act is it specified that these arrangements relate to the Christian religion, although it is stipulated that in county schools neither the act of worship nor the religious education shall be distinctive of any particular religious denomination.

Paragraph 5 of Section 25 provides for the withdrawal of pupils for the purpose of receiving outside the school religious instruction of a kind which is not provided in the school, and Section 26 makes provision under specified circumstances for

D

facilities to be made available for pupils to receive religious instruction in county schools in accordance with the tenets of a particular religious denomination.

Surveys of minority ethnic groups in schools indicate that the withdrawal rate from religious assemblies is of the order of one per cent. The withdrawal rate for each of the ethnic groups is over twice that of indigenous, and in the case of Pakistanis is over seventeen times as high. It has also been found that proportionately more secondary children than primary children are withdrawn from assembly and, as may be expected also, proportionately more junior age children than infant.

Some headteachers have had to abandon schemes for withdrawing these pupils from assembly because the children have requested that they be readmitted for social reasons or because they have been made unhappy by this arrangement. Some schools have also experimented with assemblies which carried out the letter of the law and yet were acceptable to all religions and have met with a certain measure of success. This approach should be explored further. It is interesting also to note that, although minority ethnic group parents are aware of their right to withdraw pupils from both religious assemblies and religious teaching, proportionately very few do make requests to this effect. Asian parents usually make it clear at the outset that they wish their children to participate fully in the life and worship of the school assuming, perhaps, that religious education teaching will be descriptive and not a means of induction into the Christian faith. Teachers often remark upon the religious sensitivity and feeling among Asian girls, no doubt due to their upbringing, and examination syllabuses (e.g. CSE) do allow pupils to study faiths other than Christianity. In addition, Indian girls often show a flair for dance and movement which is a traditional form of religious expression in their culture and school staff may not appreciate that dance, movement and drama can provide ways of exploring religious concepts which could form part of a religious education programme. West

Indian pupils often have a close link with church and Sunday School, so that their knowledge of biblical stories is often more extensive than that of other pupils.

Recently a group of HM inspectors carried out a survey of religious education in a number of primary and secondary multiracial schools. They found that with some exceptions the programme of religious education being followed in secondary schools consisted of a three-year course in some biblical history and theology followed by discussion of social questions. In primary schools it often contained the telling of bible stories from the synoptic gospels and the patriarchal period of Jewish history. Teachers expressed dissatisfaction with their syllabuses and yet it was found that few were aware of the content and philosophy of more recent schemes. In the agreed syllabuses of the authorities covered by the survey it was unusual to find any provision for the systematic treatment of material relating to world faiths, other than Christianity, below the sixth form. Teachers in both primary and secondary schools felt the need to deal with this subject at an earlier stage but were generally unsure of what material was suitable or how it could be used profitably.

Some answers to the foregoing are given in two articles published by the Christian Education Movement which follow.

RELIGIOUS EDUCATION IN PRIMARY SCHOOLS*
What can be taught in the primary school and how?

What can be taught depends on what one is teaching as general topics, for example, Mexico the Aztecs, India Hinduism Arabia Islam. Common sense would suggest that Judaism (not a Christianized view of the Old Testament), Hinduism, Islam, Sikhism and Buddhism will provide most if not all the content additional to Christianity for under-thirteens.

How it should be taught is largely descriptive, related to the

*Taken from *World Religions in the Primary School*, Owen Cole (published by CEM but now out of print).

children's experience. Pictures, filmstrips and books are available showing the Muslim at prayer, the Buddhist monk in his saffron robes, the Hindu bathing in the Ganges or joining in a festive procession or wedding. Description is possible and the religious life of people of other lands can be examined to the same depth that many today would advocate the teaching of Christianity at the Primary stage. Attitudes can be formed and factual information given; both are valuable and necessary pre-requisites for a study of concepts in the secondary school. Comparison in the sense of variety can be made, comparison resulting in a value judgement must be avoided.

What content is within the grasp of our primary children?

In *Hinduism:* Temples and pilgrimages: festivals – Holi and Divali: meditation and prayer: the teaching of the guru and the initiation ceremony of Upanayana: weddings.

In *Buddhism:* some of the stories of Gautama and some of his teachings: statues of the Buddha and what they represent: Temples: monks: the Shin byu ceremony of initiation.

In *Islam:* some of the stories of the life of the Prophet and the spread of Islam: Ramadhan and the Idds, Mosques, some mention of prayer and of the Koran.

References to the *Sikh religion* should include something about the life of Nanak, the five Ks and why Guru Gobind Singh introduced them, the Temple at Amritsar, perhaps the Amrit ceremony, the Free Kitchen and a Sikh wedding. The best way to introduce teaching about these religions is casually from the age of eight or nine except where, in such cities as Leeds or Birmingham, children are experiencing contact with children of these faiths from the start of their school lives. In such circumstances story-time should include the folk tales of these societies as well as those of our own. A diet of English-centred stories (including Jewish/Christian) will quickly tell children that Asian immigrants have no cultural heritage of their own worth knowing. The themes of homes, clothes and food present opportunities for infants to discover some of the details of Indian, Pakistani and West Indian life, to see the beauty of a Sari, to discover how dependent we are upon the Indian sub-continent for our food. This is not, of course, religious education, if a restricted interpretation is put upon that phrase. But then neither are flat-roofed houses and fishermen on the Sea of Galilee. Such information can stimulate interest and help children to form attitudes – that Palestine and Asia are worth knowing about and so, eventually, the ideas emanating from these religions are important.

Where there are no minority ethnic group pupils these suggestions may well seem irrelevant. Against this, three observations can be made. First, religious education in a wider than Christian sense must have a place in the primary school on its own merits, regardless of the religious heritage of the children. Soon enough children realize they are in a multi-religious world, it is better that they should be told this than find it out for themselves. Secondly, in the same way the coming of Muslims and Sikhs to places where there are now none should be anticipated. Thirdly, while the mass media are informing us of the existence of a 'Third World', we must educate our children in its cultures and ideas to show that the story is not simply one of poverty but that we have much to learn as well as give. This is the task of art and music, home economics and history as well as RE, of course, but Christianity has been largely responsible for ideas of western supremacy and RE must now help eradicate certain resultant evils. In the Junior School experiential teaching must anticipate situations, not just wait for them – otherwise most children would never be ready to learn French, and much science or craft work.

From the age of eight or nine the content outlined earlier may be used within themes such as 'light' and topics such as 'India', 'oil' or 'journeys'. To the Rupert Hart Davies booklets on 'Light' (Christian-based as most of the Goldman-inspired material is) a study of Channukkah and Divali could be added.

'Oil' and 'journeys' enable juniors to enjoy searching through atlases and making models of cars and ships. They should also permit a study of people not just how they live but how they worship, and something of the biography and ideas of such men as Mohammed. The interest children show and the deep and serious questions asked even by second-year juniors should convince even the most cautious teacher that to omit religious 'exploration' from such topics is unfair. Yet one comes across schemes and classbooks on the Crusades which seem reluctant to provide any worthwhile information about Mohammed or the Muslim faith. The impression is frequently given that chivalrous Christians defeated barbarous Saracens, which is a travesty of the truth!

Many children will be confirmed in their middle school years, this provides a natural opportunity to look at Bar Mitzvah, the Sikh Amrit ceremony or similar moments in the life of a young boy of some other faith. Summer frequently brings an excursion to an ancient monument. A ruined abbey not only presents an opportunity for stimulating enthusiasm for history, it can also encourage children to find out why people turned to this way of life and to finding out about living in contemporary Buddhist monasteries.

Problems

There are, of course, a number of problems which cannot be ignored and which must be considered before embarking upon particular aspects of the course. Hindu pictures or film strips may show deities with many arms, pot-bellied Ganeshas or effeminate looking Krishnas. These can be used to show the richness of the Hindu idea of God who is within the whole of life, small as a grain of rice, vaster than the Universe itself, so that no single idea can contain Him. Yet the Rig Veda says 'God is one though sages call him by many names'. Preraphaelite-Victorian sentimentality and a deep rooted tendency in Hinduism to see both female and male principles within deity goes some way to accounting for the apparent femininity of Siva, Krishna or Guru Nanak as a youth when depicted in art.

Hindu myths need care in the telling. Yet belong to the same type of literature as the Creation, Fall and Flood stories of the Old Testament. They convey religious ideas and should not be told as fairy tales even though some anthologies are called 'Indian Fairy Tales'. A book which may help is *Gods, Demons and Others* by Narayan (Heinemann, 1965). Judaism and Islam regard Jesus in a way Christians do not. 'Why don't Jews believe in Jesus?' is a question which should not be avoided. There is no reason why religious prudery should remain when sexual prudery has gone. Guru Nanak, the Buddha, Martin Luther and John Wesley all protested against degenerate religious practices and ideas. As Luther cannot be understood in a Vatican II context so Nanak is incomprehensible if one has Mohammed and Radhakrishnan in mind. If such a book as Mala Singh's *The Story of Guru Nanak* is given to children it must be explained that it is fair neither to Hindu nor Muslim. However, children need to learn that everyone has a point of view, that few books or teachers are objective and they must make their own search for meaning and bid for tolerance. In this exercise the study of world religions is important and a beginning can be made in the junior school. Although the main teachings and belief systems of the great religions must wait until later, because children are not yet ready to understand them, nevertheless, two of the aims outlined by Edwin Cox (*Changing Aims in Religious Education*, pp. 86–90) have been realized: interest in other religions has been aroused in such a way that a favourable attitude towards, and an interest in them has been created, and factual knowledge has been acquired. As a bonus the third aim of understanding personal relationships may have gone some way towards being satisfied. Through understanding something of their religions a basis for mutual respect between white and non-white may have been established, for [toleration cannot be built on ignorance,] nor upon the feeling of white Christian superiority which is built into our Agreed Syllabuses, the whole School curriculum and our everyday way of life.

At this juncture a word might be said about the *multi-faith primary school*. The approach here, will differ from that adopted in the school whose children all come from a Christian heritage. First, references to Islam must begin at five if there are Muslims in the school, secondly, such references must be constantly present in the themes, topics and projects done by the children. Christianty this year and next year, with Islam sometime or never cannot be expected to satisfy them. Finally, Ramadhan (Urdu-Ramzan) and the Two Idds, Passover, Jewish New Channukkah, Divali, Baisakhi and the birthdays of Guru Nanak and Guru Gobind Singh, must have a place alongside Christmas in schools which have numbers of Jewish, Muslim, Hindu and Sikh children. A two-tier approach would seem appropriate.

Tier One: 5–9 'Direct Concrete'. References to the customs, clothes, foods, holidays, homes and families, places of worship of the children in this class so that differences – not eating pork, being called Manjit or Sat Nour Singh, wearing a top knot or turban – will be recognized and regarded as acceptable not 'funny'.

Tier Two: 9–13 'Vicarious Concrete'. Similar contents can now be explored at greater depth and distance using, for example *Ramu* by Mehta (published by Angus and Watson) to describe Divali, or a 'Hindu Family in Britain', the Concordia filmstrips, visits to synagogues etc., BBC Schools broadcasts – though these often try to cover too much (the Sikhs in 20 minutes!) and include beliefs far too early. One must, of course, remember the needs of West Indian children for black examples of caring, forgiveness etc., with which they can identify.

A short bibliography for the teacher
NOSS: *Man's Religions* (Macmillan)

PARRINDER: *What World Religions Teach* (Pan)
PARRINDER: *Worship in the World's Religions* (Faber)
E. O. JAMES: *From Cave to Cathedral* (Thames and Hudson)
W. CANTWELL SMITH: *The Faith of Other Men* (Mentor Paperbacks)
K. KLOSTERMAIER: *Hindu and Christian in Vrindaban* (SCM)

A brief outline of the Sikh Faith by Mrs P. M. Wylam and a number of other useful pamphlets can be obtained from the Sikh Cultural Society, 88 Mollison Way, Edgware, Middlesex.

Probe 14 *Community Relations* by CEM is full of useful information for teachers in multi-faith schools. See also Primary Panel Mailing No. 4. CEM *R.E. in a Multi-Faith Society*.

Sons of the Laws by W. N. Carter, Olive Press, Lincoln's Inn Fields, London, W.C.2. provides helpful information on Judaism; also *Our Neighbours the Jews* by George H. Stevens (SPCK).

Further sources for ideas on teaching world religions in the primary school are:

Hinduism edited by J. Hinnells & E. J. Sharpe (Oriel Press). This primer on Hinduism also includes sections on the teaching of Hinduism in schools, colleges and universities.

Learning for Living, Jan. 1972, 'Islam' (CEM) also includes advice for the teacher.

World Religions: Aids for Teachers produced by the SHAP Working Party for Community Relations Commission contains some book lists relevant to primary school R.E.

Books for children: *The Homelands of Immigrants in Britain*, edited by Janet Hill, Institute of Race Relations, 247–9, Pentonville Road, London N.1, contains annotated and graded book lists for primary children.

RELIGIOUS EDUCATION IN SECONDARY SCHOOLS

The following suggested R.E. syllabus is quoted from the CEM paper on *World Religions in the Secondary School*, by Donald Butler.

(*a*) The aims for this particular scheme of work are:

(i) To provide pupils with opportunities to explore religious experience': i.e. to meet and respond to the situations which the world's religions present, and to learn something about what it means to be members of some of the great religious traditions and cultures.

(ii) To help pupils to become mature in 'religious thinking': i.e. to be able to make valid and sincere value judgements on religious matters, and thereby to become mature and well-motivated members of our plural society.

(iii) To suggest to pupils that Religious Studies is a thoroughly respectable choice for CSE or GCE, and later, for a main course at college or university.

(iv) To leave the pupil with a life long respect for religion, and for religious people.

(*b*) The syllabus outline at a glance:

FIRST YEAR (11+) What is Christianity?

SECOND YEAR (12+) The story of the Jews.

THIRD YEAR (13+) Great Religions of the World.

FOURTH YEAR (14+) Me and my World.

FIFTH YEAR (15+) Us and our World.

SIXTH FORM Religious questions in the context of General Studies.

This section makes no attempt to discuss examination courses for CSE or GCE. Each of these headings will be discussed in the light of the following questions:

1 What does this really mean, and what does it involve? (TITLE)

2 What topics might be included, and how are they useful for the pupils? (TOPICS.)

3. How should these topics be presented? (METHOD)

4 What books and other aids are there, for the teacher and pupils who are just embarking on these topics for the first time? (AIDS)

(c) Three good sources of information about teaching aids of all kinds:

(i) SHAP Working Party, Borough Road College, Isleworth, Middlesex.

(ii) Secretary for the International Dept., CEM.

(iii) The Community Relations Commission, 15 Bedford Street, London, WC2.

(d) A footnote about 'threads, themes and units'.

Threads: Ideally, religion should be treated as a global study, with the pupil frequently being made aware of the universal nature of the subject. One way of achieving this is to weave a thread of world religion content into the fabric of the traditional topics. For instance, the gospel narratives easily provide opportunities to study the religions of ancient Greece and Rome, Mithraism and Zoroastrianism, and the cult of the Essenes.

Themes: A class embarking on a good thematic approach, say, to a Christian topic like the family, or festivals, can derive real 'religious experience' from seeing the theme in question through the eyes of a non-Christian too, especially as there are non-Christians in this country who are obliged to see our western/Christian customs 'from the outside.'

Units: Pupils of 13 + are ready for a businesslike, thorough approach to World Religions. They feel that they want to have 'something to show' for their time spent in study. They actually *like* having at least the main characteristics of a new religion or culture set out for them. It is not so much that they want to compare one religion with another: in fact, comparisons are in general to be avoided, since we are teaching topics which gain very little from being compared, and may indeed be the victims of grave misunderstanding if comparison is imposed upon them. What young teenagers do enjoy is the feeling that they have been properly introduced to a new religion, and can speak authoritatively about it. This can best be done by presenting the major religions as self-contained units. Perhaps it would be as well to add that it is by no means the aim of this syllabus to produce 'world religion experts'! But that is no reason to do less than provide a good working knowledge, and thereby the material, for aims set out above.

(e) A footnote about the school assembly.

It is not the aim here to make suggestions about World Religions and the school or house assembly. However it is worth observing that if the assembly is seen as the occasion when pupils, gathered in a natural corporate body, may hear or see assembly material which will catch their imagination, and come to mind as they proceed through the daily routine of the school, then there is no reason why that material should not be derived from any religious tradition, or from Humanist or secular material. In fact, pupils are likely to give more than a passing thought to ideas which are presented to them from an unfamiliar or unlikely source.

(f) It should not need to be said that whatever the teacher's own views are about the topics contained in this syllabus, the world's religions are the deeply held and respected views of religious men and women, and of children too, for that matter, and should be treated as such.

The CEM article then continues and develops each of the year syllabuses in considerable detail and also indicates the relevant resources available to both the teacher and pupils.

FURTHER RESOURCES

CONCORDIA films (117, Golden Lane, London EC1) has produced coloured filmstrips on the main religions of the world. In addition there is a BBC 'Religion in its contemporary context' series. This is a radio-vision production intended for sixth formers but selected frames (and any film-strip must be used selectively) are useful. The teacher who possesses little knowledge of some of these religions will profit from studying the BBC series for himself.

COLE, W. O. (ed.) (1973) *The Multi-Faith School* (Bradford Educational Services, 31–39 Piccadilly, Bradford).

HOLROYDE, Peggy, *et al.* (1970, 2nd ed. 1973) *East Comes West: A Background to Some Asian Faiths* (Community Relations Commission).

Multi-cultural education through a school subject: Home Economics

I am quoting in this section an article by Yvonne Collymore (*Housecraft*, January 1974) which seems to me to illustrate very well the way in which an individual subject in the curriculum can play an important part in integrating immigrant children into the school community – and eventually into the wider community.

A number of teachers believe that some of the behavioural problems which they encounter with these pupils are due to the alienation which they feel at school because of their foreign culture, looks and speech, and also their alienation at home when they inevitably begin to adopt the attitudes, speech and dress of their peers. Curricula, textbooks, attitudes of staff and other pupils force them to adapt because there is often little adaptation by the school to suit the needs of the immigrant child. Some teachers have made great efforts to change this state of affairs and to adapt the syllabus to suit the needs of all the children in their classes. They have used imagination to encourage and guide the introduction of West Indian, Indian, African, Greek and Chinese foods into their lessons and have applied the basic principles of cookery and nutrition to them. Some of the difficulties encountered are listed below:

I. LACK OF KNOWLEDGE

Most found themselves almost totally ignorant of the diets and food patterns of their 'foreign' pupils. 'I had heard of yams', said one young teacher, 'but had never seen or tasted, much less cooked one, so how could I be sure when it was done?' . . . 'It bothers me', [another] said, 'that my girls never seem to eat any green vegetables in school. They say that such things are not eaten in the West Indies, yet in your book there are photographs of green vegetables and instructions for cooking them.' So the teachers realize that the pupils themselves may not be an accurate source of information, even though they may not be deliberately trying to deceive the teacher. In this case it appeared to be a good dodge for avoiding something which they dislike! . . .

2. ATTITUDES AND MISCONCEPTIONS

Many home economics teachers will admit to prejudices towards certain foods, be they kidneys, hearts, liver, fish roes, anchovies, brains or spinach. How much more widespread are the prejudices against 'funny foreign foods'. Some people genuinely cannot bear the smell of garlic or curry while others are really upset by oily or spicy dishes. How do such people react to Greek and Pakistani cooking going on in the same room at the same time as soused herrings? If they are reluctant to taste their pupils' cooking, are they encouraging and teaching? Can they hope to communicate successfully with West Indians if they believe that cat meat is really part of the West Indian diet? If teachers can acknowledge their own prejudices, can they then understand the reluctance of the Pakistani or Jamaican girl, used to highly seasoned foods when expected to eat steak and kidney pudding cooked without herbs and spices?

3. RELIGION AND FOOD

Jews settled in this country in large numbers so long ago that now it is an accepted thing for Jewish children to observe their religious feast and fast days. Yet many cookery teachers have no knowledge of Jewish food and customs. Do we really understand the meaning of Kosher meat and fats? Is it too difficult a jump from this to the Halal meat of the Muslims which, for religious reasons, must be killed with special ceremony? If we are ignorant of the Hindu and Muslim religions, how can we understand when a Ugandan Asian says that she is not allowed to eat beef or a Pakistani refuses to handle pork or bacon? Do we care that during the fast of Ramadan strict Muslims are forbidden to eat between sunrise and sunset or do we force pupils to have lunch in the housecraft room because it is their group's turn? Surely as teachers and educators our task is to educate ourselves so that we can better educate our pupils? We can ask our pupils to help by talking to us about their beliefs and customs.

4. LACK OF BOOKS AND MATERIALS

Even when busy hard-pressed teachers are eager to educate themselves further, where do they turn to look for materials? With no books and teaching aids to help, it is perhaps the brave or foolhardy who embarks on group work which gives the pupils free choice, for it is difficult to scan recipes the week before, or check quantities of ingredients before shopping takes place, if the dish is entirely unfamiliar. How will I know whether the dishes chosen can be cooked in the time available? You may wonder. With another class following on immediately this could be a problem. There is also no way of knowing if the dish has turned out well.

It is easy to see how a faint-hearted teacher can excuse herself from the ranks of the pioneers. If others can make the mistakes and pave the way she may be willing to learn and to follow suit. Understandably, the demands of timetables, examination syllabuses, finance and lack of equipment are already such headaches that to begin something which involves more organization, more time and greater expenditure of funds is off-putting to any well-intentioned teacher. Also, where classes are split it is inadvisable to cover different ground from that of your colleagues.

But those teachers who have succeeded despite the difficulties are convinced that the effort is really worthwhile, and are proud of their results. Now at least two official bodies are attempting to analyse what material is required and to produce some of it: the Inner London Education Authority Working Party on Home Economics Teaching and the Community Relations Council. Teachers' centres are attempting to do all they can and publishers are beginning to recognize the existence of a demand. [These publications are available from the ILEA Media Resources Centre, Highbury Station Road, London N1. *Author*.]

5. OPPOSITION TO MULTI-CULTURAL TEACHING

There are many strong arguments militating against special considerations for the immigrant school community. Some teachers maintain that second generation immigrants have no interest in the cookery of their 'home' country and that trying to foster an interest only isolates them still further by making them feel 'different'. Some argue that it is unfair to the indigenous English children to pay so much attention to the children of immigrants from the New Commonwealth – especially when the newcomers are in the minority. If they want to live in this country they should be prepared to adopt our habits and customs, say others. There is the argument, accepted by some immigrant parents, that the continuance of cultural patterns is the responsibility of the parent. However, as a West Indian, who came to this country as a child, I should like to argue in favour of schools fostering this interest, with parents doing their part. Sooner or later in this society the immigrant child is made aware of the fact that he or she is different. What the schools can do to help is to make children realize that being different does not necessarily mean being inferior, and that a knowledge and understanding of two cultures can enrich and make them not only different but special people with more to offer. For the indigenous English child it is now accepted that being part of a European Community offers wider opportunity for learning and experience, and I would like to suggest that widening his or her experiences still further to take in the ancient cultures of India, Africa, and China can do nothing but good.

But if we disregard cookery and look at the other aspects of home economics: good grooming, dress and appearance, community and family life; social behaviour, morals, sex education and child care, how much relevance does our teaching bear to the lives of our immigrant pupils? Is it so far removed from reality that it will be simply something learned in school and forgotten outside? How can a West Indian girl with African looks, hair, and colour relate the information on hair care and make-up to her own complexion, skin and hair texture? Surely at this point she must realize that she is different and the teaching irrelevant?

Moreover I believe that home economics has a great part to play in the assimilation of these children into the school community and later into society. Through this subject they learn some of the customs and social habits of English society and also some of the values and conflicts. For non-English speakers it is one of the lessons in which they can participate whilst learning the language. For all, whether there is some understanding of the language or not, it is a means of enlarging vocabulary and experience, and teachers can help very much here with language teaching and reading for information ... (Yvonne Collymore, *Housecraft*, January 1974).

Physical Education

Many of the difficulties facing teachers of this subject may only occur in certain aspects e.g. swimming, dancing, gymnastics etc.

E

Many girls still wear national costume except for Physical Education when these clothes would be unsuitable and dangerous. However, there is still a reluctance by many to remove the shulwar as there is also to taking part in, for example, country dancing when the class is mixed. Many will not participate unless the class is single sex. Asian girls, especially Moslems are, reluctant to change for PE and furthermore to strip for a shower. The latter difficulty is overcome in some schools by allowing the girls to change into swimsuits in the lavatory cubicles before showering. However, it is interesting that some headteachers of inner city schools often comment that the housing conditions of both immigrant and indigenous children are so bad that showers are often welcomed.

Many Moslem Asian girls are not allowed to swim; for cultural and religious reasons it is unsuitable for them to do so. While they are at primary school the objection is not so serious, but when they reach puberty at secondary school their parents often insist that they should be excused for swimming lessons. Two reasons for this objection are the risk of the girl being seen by a man while inadequately covered, and the impurity of the pool water. After swimming in a pool the girl would have to wash and change before being able to enter a mosque and touch the Koran. As it is the custom to attend the mosque almost directly after school, this would be inconvenient.

Discipline problems

It is often remarked that West Indian pupils can be disruptive in a school; and one of the reasons put forward for this is that of cultural difference between the present English and the West Indian attitude to discipline. West Indian home discipline is often quoted as being harsh, firm and repressive – involving beating, belting and the strap. In contrast to this, the majority of teachers in the English educational system see discipline as involving self-discipline, liberal attitudes, tolerance and a certain amount of informality; though one ought to remember that this has not always been the prevalent attitude. Often West Indian parents and children interpret the more 'liberal' attitude to discipline as weakness. Having said this, one must add that negative generalizations of this kind need to be interpreted cautiously. In the case of children's behaviour in the classroom it is often the extreme cases which provide the stereotypes, and in the case of home discipline, while most West Indian parents are certainly strict, they may overestimate their own severity when talking with teachers. Not only West Indian, but also Asian and Italian children, often experience much stricter discipline at home than indigenous pupils, and they may consequently find it more difficult to adjust to the comparatively lax discipline in their school. One quite often hears of West Indian and Asian parents asking the school to exert physical discipline on their children, and indeed some West Indian parents appear to subscribe to the view that beating a child will improve his learning.

The differences of attitude between parents and school teachers towards child rearing have their effect. It has been reported by teachers that the disparity manifests itself in children in bewilderment, difficulty in settling down to life in the classroom, and in attempts to take advantage of the more lenient atmosphere of the school. When this happens teachers are faced with the dilemma of whether or not to report the child's misbehaviour to his parents. The resultant 'good hiding' may help restore order in the classroom, but will most likely destroy the fine balance of understanding needed in good teacher–pupil relationships.

The West Indian pattern of family life is often referred to as a possible cause of disturbance amongst pupils. Many West Indian pupils have not seen their parents for many years, having been brought up in the West Indies by a grandmother and only later joining their mother and father (or step-father) in England. They may also have to get used to living with brothers and sisters never met before. Certain 'unacceptable' behaviour is caused by different cultural values, norms and expectations.

Though the atmosphere and equipment of an English primary school might be considered adequate for certain kinds of learning, nevertheless immigrant pupils may be bemused not only by the permissive attitude of their teacher, but also overwhelmed by the decoration, and profusion of equipment. It is known that some children react by rushing from one activity to another; or alternatively they may feel threatened rather than stimulated by the environment, and react by being reserved and introverted. They seem in these cases to be frightened by the freedom of choice, and find it impossible to make any choice at all (cf. Schools Council Working Paper 31: *Immigrant Children in Infant Schools*, Evans/Methuen Educational, 1970).

Some research undertaken by the Schools Council and others (e.g. Bhatnagar, *Immigrants at School*, Cornmarket Press, 1970) has tended to confirm the impressions gained by teachers from their own experience. Among the findings of the Schools Council research was the indication that West Indian children aged eight to nine acted more aggressively, anxiously and restlessly than other groups, and had less concern for adult approval. It was also reported that West Indian children of twelve to thirteen years of age showed more hostility towards adults than did other groups. (This research is reported in Paul Widlake's *The Multiracial Class*, Evans, 1973.) Bhatnagar found a considerable difference in levels of adjustment between English and immigrant secondary school children.

Though we may feel inclined to accept, as a result of these sorts of research findings and our own experience, that a minority of West Indian pupils (for example) will behave disruptively in school, and though we may also recognize that many minority ethnic group children may have learning difficulties, yet these perceptions need not overinfluence our outlook. Paul Widlake (op. cit.) has said: 'let us avoid generalizations and typings and view [the children] simply as human beings placed in an indisputable adverse social situation.' If we do not do this it is all too easy for both us and our pupils to react with fear and hostility, which will certainly not help either the teaching or the learning process. It would be more profitable, perhaps, for teachers to concentrate upon achievement within ethnic groups rather than focus, as often happens, on the differences between groups. Progress would perhaps be easier in the multiracial classroom if we could concentrate more on signs of potential and less on evidence of difference and of behaviour problems.

School meals

Proportionately fewer Asian immigrant children stay for school dinners than indigenous children, either because of dietary considerations or because they live near the school and few Asian mothers go out to work. However, the parents of those children that *do* stay, often request vegetarian meals or meals without certain types of meat. Some teachers have been very concerned about the reluctance of some Asian children to eat the vegetable meals that are provided as an alternative to meat dishes. Feeling that lack of sustenance at school together with the lack of a balanced diet at home might injure such children's health, some school doctors prescribe vitamin tablets. Many infant teachers, in particular, stress the necessity for free school milk and vitamin deficiency tablets for young immigrant children.

It is the tradition among Indians and Pakistanis that food is eaten with the fingers only, or with the help of a chapatti (pancake). This approach is therefore not bad manners although teachers brought up in this country might possibly mistake it for such. Those children who stay to school dinners may at first require guidance in the use of cutlery. Pakistanis who are practising Muslims do not eat pork. They are often very sensitive on this subject and a picture, story or nursery rhyme about pigs could be extremely offensive to them. In addition it is worth noting that Sikhs and Hindus usually decline to eat beef or even food cooked in animal fat.

A further dietary problem as far as the schools are concerned, is that Moslem children observe a dawn to dusk fast during the Muslim month of fast (Ramadan). At the end of a month without lunches all aspects of a child's performance may deteriorate.

Extra-curricular activities

Asian pupils may show a reluctance to join in any extra-curricular activities, possibly because they do not appreciate the educative value of school journeys, regarding them more as social occasions. In addition such outings may prompt Asian parents to raise questions concerning food and sleeping arrangements. Because of the system of 'arranged marriages' many Indian girls are not allowed to participate in activities involving both boys and girls which are organized after school hours. However teachers have often found that Indian fathers are agreeable after consultation and explanations, and request special arrangements without appreciating the difficulty of making these from a financial point of view though, in fact, the father's agreement often proves empty because the mother, who remains at home and takes no part in the discussion with the teacher, will not grant the plan her blessing. When Asian pupils do manage to attend functions outside school hours they have been found to be sociable and popular.

For West Indians participation in out-of-school activities is often difficult because their home commitments are heavy. Often both parents are working during the day (or one at night and one during the day). Hence the elder children have to accept responsibility for certain domestic chores, baby-sitting, etc. Perhaps if teachers could improve their contact with the children's parents and persuade them to accept the educational value of such school outings and events, this situation might be altered. Other arrangements could possibly be made at home so that the children could get the chance to join in more extra-curricular activities.

Co-education

In their own society Asian girls have been taught to avoid male company from about the age of ten upwards, and they settle more readily in English schools if seated with other girls in the classroom. It is common for Asian parents to desire single-sex secondary education for their children, though to what extent Asian immigrants choose single-sex schools, where these are available, in preference to mixed schools when their children transfer from primary to secondary, is not known. With our different social customs it may be hard for us to appreciate the importance of such matters, and we might feel inclined to smile at stories such as that of the father of an eleven-year-old Indian boy who requested his son's transfer from a mixed to a boys' high school on the grounds that it was his (the father's) duty to choose a wife for his son, and no risk must be taken of the son's choosing his own.

Teachers may well find that Asian immigrant pupils them-selves object to co-education, and boys may not wish to sit with girls, and vice versa. Linked to this attitude, at times, is a certain lack of respect on the part of Indian boys for women teachers, especially young ones, and (occasionally) for English girls.

However, as with many other traditional customs, single-sex education is dying out in India. Thus it would not neces-sarily be in the interests of Indian pupils, and might prove confusing, to make extraordinary efforts to reconcile our edu-cational arrangements and their preferences. The same might apply to certain preferences of other minority ethnic groups. In other words it would be helpful sometimes if the protagonists in the 'integration debate' reminded themselves that often traditional customs are upheld mainly by those who have left the country where those customs originated.

Clothing

Many Pakistani girls and those from Northern India wear shulwar-kamiz (tunic and trousers), while other Indian girls wear saris, and a few older ones may wear veils. Sikh boys are obliged by their faith to wear turbans, which also keep their uncut hair tidy. Most schools would prefer their children to appear in European dress and attempt to wean the Asians from the customs which interfere most with school practice. However, these traditions are deeply rooted and the weaning process needs to be gradual. For example, many Asian girls made suddenly to bare their arms and legs in the presence of boys would feel that their reputation and marriage chances were spoiled. It is helpful, as previously mentioned when discussing Physical Education, if older girls are allowed a little time before being persuaded to change into PE kit, and if boys' and girls' swimming classes can be held separately at first. Many schools do permit the wearing of shulwars and in many cases Asian girls have dressed in the school colours in their effort to conform to the schools' requirements. Some schools allow slacks, trousers or coloured tights in place of the shulwar. Schools often specify the colour of shulwar, white being a favourite choice, and some have designed uniforms with this in mind. In the same spirit of compromise, Sikh boys have been allowed to wear turbans, once again in school colours, and have sometimes been encouraged to do so because of their long hair. In addition they often wear the ceremonial shorts, comb and bangle but not the traditional knife, or 'kirpan' which in any case is usually worn only by strictly orthodox Sikhs, and then in the form of a 'chota kirpan'.

In connection with schools' attitudes to the clothing and appearance of their minority ethnic group pupils, one ought to be aware that often the sartorial or cosmetic inclination which is seen as 'problematic' is the outcome of an attitude which is welcomed and admired. Thus the eye make-up, ear-rings and bangles of Indian girls, which cause such havoc with school regulations, are an aspect of their pious repect for religion and tradition, which may well be regarded as something excellent.

One more difficulty which many teachers experience with minority ethnic groups and clothing, is that often pupils wear clothes with a lack of regard for our climate. Thus one might find Indian pupils wearing too little and Italians wearing too much. This has been observed most often by primary school teachers.

Contributions made by minority ethnic groups

We have been discussing some of the problems and challenges that may face the teacher in a multiracial school, but there is no doubt that there are also many advantages to a school or class which contains pupils from different countries and backgrounds. The advantages for schools, both primary and secondary, may best be illustrated by quoting from H. E. R. Townsend and E. M. Brittan, *Organization in Multiracial Schools* (NFER, 1972, pp. 113–15):

> 'Immigrant pupils contribute to the life of the school in a thousand different ways during the course of the year'.

While many of these ways are mentioned specifically by headteachers the majority fall into the following categories: contributions to dance, music and movement; drama; art and craft; physical education; gymnastics; athletics; games; assembly and religious education lessons; geography and social studies; and to project-work in general. Typical of such comments are:

> 'The fact that we have several nationalities provides us with a colourful and lively community and leads to many projects to do with countries of origin, e.g. journeys, customs, cultures, music and dancing, etc.'

> 'The traditional and religious festivals of these immigrant

E*

children are extremely interesting and useful aids to projects on their countries, e.g. the Moslem Eid-du-Fitz, the Sikh festival of Guru Singh, the Hindu Divali and the Sikh Guru Nanak's birthday. The children bring <u>an insight into life and customs of other lands in a most vivid way.</u>'

Other comments include the following:

'The increased varieties of party celebrations and festivals both religious and social (the reasons for and nature of these) provide a stimulus to language and widening of knowledge and interest to others.'

'Our physical education has changed to accept dance and movement, e.g. limbo and Afro rhythms, etc. We also have Greek dancing and choral singing from Cyprus.'

'Their considerable musical ability and response to rhythm enliven our music and movement.'

'The West Indian and African immigrants are generally very gifted physically: some are outstanding athletes and games players.'

'In drama there is no need for us to black faces or hunt for eastern costumes.'

'In needlework they contribute work that is different both in design and in craftsmanship.'

'The Pakistani, Sikh and West Indian boys have a vigour and courage which has contributed to the school's success in inter-school (sports) competitions. Their religions teach 'charity' . . . and they are outstanding workers for all school giving.'

'The gentleness of the Indian and Pakistani girls and their air of quiet happiness have a salutary effect on the other children.'

'The simple domestic habits of West Indians—their emphasis on cleaning, cooking, needlework, etc.—are reflected in children's activities and contribute to worth-while activities with less able children in particular.'

'The warmth and ebullience of the West Indian character has enriched our school – we seem so alive! This helps other children, including some West Indians themselves who are withdrawn and moody.'

'The immigrant children help the English children to achieve the concept of a multiracial society in which they are destined to live and work during their adult life.'

The last quotation on this topic must be from the headteacher of a junior school where immigrants comprised 82 per cent of the school roll:

'No specific contribution – they are the school!'

At the secondary level the positive approaches outlined above are continually found. Some headteachers mention contributions to music and dance either in the way of enrichment of lessons or by means of extra-curricular activities, performance at school concerts, prize days, open evenings, international evenings and so on. One school mentioned the more unusual activity of having an Indian boys' dance group. Contributions to art and craft work were also mentioned a number of times, for example:

'Their nature and national flair for colour and design has produced some highly unusual and decorative pieces of art and craft which act as an inspiration to others.'

Needlework, metalwork and woodwork are also mentioned, as is also home economics:

'Girls contribute by demonstrating their national dishes to illustrate various skills and food values.'

After music and dance, one of the most frequently mentioned areas of school life is that of physical education:

'The greatest contribution is in physical activities and games. To association football, hockey, cricket and athletics our immigrants make a tremendous contribution. They are generally poor at competitive swimming and do not take well to rugby football, especially the Asians. The latter are, however, outstanding at road walking. They also do well at basketball, fencing and dancing!'

A small number of headteachers also mention Geography and History:

'Immigrant pupils make a real contribution to Geography lessons, particularly the Asians from Kenya, the Sudan and the Congo, The West Indians are not very forthcoming.'

Contributions to religious education are mentioned only briefly and some headteachers report contributions in the way of social service, help being given to the aged and sick, for example, and entertainment to people in hospital.

A different kind of conbribution is often mentioned by a number of headteachers:

'Dignity of learning and courtesy which grow out of a strong family unit and, linked with this, a praiseworthy attitude towards work';

'The manners and dress of most Indians are a credit to the school and their parents.'

'Respect for educational opportunities, knowledge, skills, and authority . . .'

'The keenness and industry of the majority of Indians is a good example to non-immigrants.'

'Cheerfulness and courtesy.'

And finally:

'It is, I believe, largely due to our immigrant families, who are fiercely determined to obtain for their children the best value possible from our educational system, that we have, in this culturally deprived area, a developing fifth and sixth year. The high standard of co-operation in the school vouch-safed by our immigrant families is . . . a great encouragement to us all.'

Conclusion

Most of the 'problems' discussed in this chapter arise from cultural and religious differences between minority ethnic groups and the host community. Undoubtedly, too, official tardiness in spotting and acting on educational difficulties of immigrants, and racist attitudes which still exist in our society, have not helped pupils and teachers in multiracial schools. Greater understanding is needed on both sides. I think it is important that there should be as much contact between schools and parents as possible, and that the aims of the school should be made clear to parents. Improved contact will help remove suspicion and, hopefully, encourage a more open attitude of mind on both sides so that genuine discussions on 'problems' can result in genuinely appreciated solutions.

6

The teacher's contribution towards education for a multicultural society

Unquestionably Britain is a multicultural society, although this is much more apparent in our urban than our rural areas. However, through hearing the political debate over immigration policy and receiving information via the mass media most people in Britain are well aware of the facts, an awareness which had been increased by comparatively recent changes in the racial composition of our society. The population of Britain now includes one and a half million of the largest minority ethnic groups in addition to others, almost half of whom were born here. The future development of British society depends to a considerable degree upon the kind of education these children receive and it follows logically from such an assertion that the training of teachers and other professionals involved should prepare them to work in, and make a positive contribution towards, the development of such a society. This book has, albeit in a limited manner, attempted to offer guidelines indicating those areas of knowledge which are necessary for teachers. Obviously it is not enough merely to have knowledge of facts, and the development of social skills, (to take but one example), is equally vital for teachers in multiracial schools. Seeing that the effectiveness of the teacher's contribution towards education for a multicultural society will obviously rely heavily on his ability to cope with the ever-increasing changes in our society, he (or she) must be able to relate meaningfully to a wide range of people, to recognize and confront personal prejudices and finally to recognize his own needs both as a teacher and an individual and to take effective steps to fulfil them.

What are the skills required in such a professional? They will undoubtedly include an understanding of the pupils as individuals and of the many factors which effect their development; the ability to help in establishing a school community in which, through its curriculum activities and social relationships, the development of these children will be fostered. Teachers therefore will not be primarily concerned with new sets of skills but rather with the extension of existing ones. It has become increasingly evident to those working in the field of education that 'education for a multiracial society' should take place in all schools. As a result of a joint resolution by the National Federation of ATEPO (now the National Association for Multiracial Education: NAME) and the National Union of Teachers, the Schools Council commissioned a major research project from NFER. (April 1973–December 1976) to provide material to prepare all pupils for life in a multiracial society and to meet the specific needs of multiracial classes. There are obviously considerable dangers in an ethnocentric curriculum, as emphasized in a recent joint report[1] by the CRC and the ATCDE in which they say (pp. 17–18):

Whenever and wherever student teachers eventually teach, regardless of age range or type of child, they will be involved in making curriculum choices. Therefore, all students need to be given an opportunity to consider carefully the inherent attitudes and assumptions contained in the subject matter they teach and its manner of presentation. Highly ethnocentric and implicitly biased views may be transmitted to children, both in obvious ways such as teaching about countries from which migrants have come, and also less directly but nevertheless damagingly through the attitudes communicated by other subject specialists. Such teaching can both confirm attitudes in all-white classes and aggravate difficulties of identity and confidence for children from minority ethnic groups. On the other hand, as has already been indicated, the curriculum can provide excellent opportunities for presenting other cultures and highlighting the achievements of all human groups.

It is obviously of considerable importance that all teachers become sensitive to and appreciative of this function of the curriculum. It has been suggested that since the minority ethnic groups have come to live permanently in Britain they should be prepared to abandon their cultural heritage and identify with the host community. This attitude gives rise to a view that schools should inculcate/indoctrinate minority ethnic group children with a 'ready-to-wear' set of British concepts and values in order to ease their entry into our society and eventually to promote assimilation. This view has gained considerable support, but it remains a simple fact that a school can only, and must, build on what is there, and this presupposes that the teacher is fully aware of the children's backgrounds. In this connection it is of paramount importance that teachers encourage a positive and receptive attitude to learning and the achievement of the latter is impossible when the children have negative self images. To quote the CRC/ATCDE report again (p. 18):

It would seem that integration must involve not an eradication of differences, but a harmonious synthesis of and respect for differences. In such a situation education will have to take account of how to ensure that all children form an adequate image of themselves and their community and that the prejudices of society at large are challenged. Many teachers in training are critical of the curriculum they followed and of that they find in some schools, they are eager to teach more relevantly for contemporary society, and if made aware of the curriculum implications of teaching in a multi-cultural society such students are likely to respond.

Educationally schools must take some initiative to promote understanding for minority ethnic groups and their British children in our increasingly multiracial society. Although there are many multiracial schools, we do not know how many have the types of social studies curricula outlined for example, by McNeal and Rogers (1971):[2] courses which should be in the curricula of all schools. Many of these developments have of course, been reported for example in the CRC's monthly bulletin, *Education and Community Relations*. In addition there are also more books and bibliographies now available to enable teachers to develop such courses.

The number of syllabuses which aim to provide the essential background to an intelligent study of racial, religious and cultural differences has also increased. Some have been devised by teachers in multiracial schools in, for example, Social Studies teaching and CSE Religious Studies syllabuses. The Scottish Modern Studies syllabus is devoted wholly to multiracial societies. UNESCO programmes are also designed to promote international understanding. Townsend's (1973)[3] third study gives us further details of successful practices and the Schools Council curriculum projects on Religious Education, General Studies, Moral Education and the Humanities include the topics of race and multiracial relations in their syllabuses.

There is an increasing number of Black Studies courses with the emphasis on the history of the particular groups. For example, at Tulse Hill Comprehensive School in South London 'Black Studies' is offered as one of three options for 'O' Level GCE in General Studies. An outline of some of the topics covered by such courses is described in issues of *Education and*

Community Relations (1971) and by Pollack, (1972)[4] and ranges widely through the social and cultural patterns of the West Indians, Africans, South Americans, Afro-Americans and Asians.

It is anticipated that such courses and action will improve the self-image of minority ethnic group children and promote respect for other cultures in the host society. This is essential for the children in all communities in Britain, whether or not minority ethnic groups live in the children's own environment.

In making these comments and reflecting upon the remainder of the book I am aware that the reader may be left with the feeling that little has been achieved. To leave such an impression would be unfair to all those teachers who quietly and efficiently rose to the challenge of new and untested circumstances amidst considerable difficulties, of which the general public were unaware. To quote Townsend and Brittan, there has had to be 'a constant adaptation of tried and tested procedures to untried and untested circumstances that speaks volumes for the flexibility of the teaching profession'.[15] It has of course been suggested that the slow growth of minority ethnic groups in this country during the past two decades has been a major factor in this adaptation but it may also have been the major cause of many residual difficulties. If we had had prior knowledge of the numbers of minority ethnic group children who are currently in our schools then our organization would not be as it is today. However it is not (and must not be) too late now to prepare for future new arrivals from overseas and those born here.

It is appropriate at the end of this book that acknowledgement should be made of the many and varied changes that minority ethnic group families have made in their traditional way of life to meet what must appear to them to be the incomprehensible demands of the English educational system. In this respect differences between groups always tend to be more obvious and exaggerated, than similarities, the occasional turban being more readily recognized as an 'immigrant' characteristic than is the general acceptance of and conformity to school uniform.

Those readers who have lived in the West Indies, India or Pakistan will appreciate how much the adaptation of British schools to a multiracial role has been more than equalled by the unassuming adaptation of minority ethnic group parents and children to our education system.

References

1 *Teacher Education for a Multi-cultural Society*. A joint report by the CRS and ATCDE (1974).
2 MCNEAL, J. and ROGERS, M. (1971) (eds) *The Multi-Racial School*. Penguin (Education).
3 TOWNSEND, H. E. R. (1973) *Multiracial Education. Need and Innovation*. Schools Council Working Paper 50. Evans/Methuen Educational.
4 POLLACK, M. (1972) A suggested black studies syllabus. *Teachers Against Racism*, June.
5 TOWNSEND, H. E. R. and BRITTAN, E. M. (1972) *Organization in Multiracial Schools*. NFER.

Aids for
the teacher

Journals

Among journals of particular relevance are:

CRC Journal
Bi-monthly journal of the Community Relations
Commission. Published by the Community Relations
Commission, 15/16 Bedford Street, London WC2.

Education and Community Relations
Monthly education bulletin published by the Community
Relations Commission.

Language Teaching and Community Relations
Quarterly bulletin for adult language teaching.
Published by the Community Relations Commission.

Multiracial School
Formerly *English for Immigrants* (3 per annum). Published
by the National Association for Multiracial Education.

New Community
Quarterly journal of the Community Relations
Commission.

Race

A quarterly journal published by the Institute of Race Relations, 249/279 Pentonville Road, London N1.

Race Today

Fortnightly journal published by Towards Racial Justice, 74 Shakespeare Road, SE24 0PP.

Runnymede Trust Bulletin

Monthly bulletin published by the Runnymede Trust, Stuart House, 1 Tudor Street, London EC4Y 0AD.

Teacher Education and Community Relations

Termly bulletin published by the Community Relations Commission.

Audio-Visual Aids

Useful indexes covering audio-visual aids are:

1 CELPIS (Colleges of Education Learning Programmes Information Service). This lists some audio-visual materials made by colleges and departments of education. Particularly relevant headings in the first edition are *Education 371–67* 'Special Education – Immigrants': and 428.24 'English as a second language – Immigrants'.

2 HELPIS (Higher Education Learning Programmes Information Service). This covers some audio-visual materials made by higher and further education institutions. It is arranged in classified order and has a subject index.

The following organizations and firms hire out or sell relevant films and tapes.

BBC Enterprises Film Hire,
25 The Boroughs,
Hendon,
London NW4.

British Film Institute Distribution Library,
42/43 Lower Marsh,
London SE1.

Central Film Library,
Government Building,
Broomyard Avenue,
London w3.

Community Relations Commission,
15–16 Bedford Street,
London wc2.

Concord Films Council Ltd,
Nacton,
Ipswich,
IP10 0JZ.

The Other Cinema,
12 Little Newport Street,
London wc2.

Open University,
Walton Hall,
Milton Keynes,
MK7 6AA.

Useful addresses

1 Commonwealth Institute,
Library and Resource Centre,
Kensington High Street,
London w8 6NQ.

The Library and Resource Centre of the Commonwealth
Institute has a wide range of loan material to stimulate interest
in the contemporary Commonwealth. It has material on race
relations and education in multiracial schools as well as on the
Commonwealth and associated topics. The material is in various
formats. There are books, pamphlets, periodical articles, wall
charts, wall maps, illustrations, study kits, samples of products,
35 mm filmstrips, slide sets, overhead projector transparencies,
tape recordings, cassette recordings and records.

The Library and Resource Centre is open from 10.00 a.m. to 5.30 p.m., Monday to Saturday, and visitors are encouraged to come and select their own materials if possible. A librarian is always available to give advice when required. The loan scheme is free; users pay any return postage.

2 Community and Race Relations Unit (CRRU)
  British Council of Churches,
  10 Eaton Gate,
  London SW1W 9BT.

CRRU is concerned with education and guidance in the field of community and race relations. It encourages Christian and local community projects in the UK. The unit has produced a number of publications; details on request.

3 Community Relations Commission (CRC)
  15/16 Bedford Street,
  London WC2.

The Community Relations Commission was established under the Race Relations Act 1968. Under the Act it has the broad duties:

(a) to encourage the establishment of, and assist others to take steps to secure the establishment of, harmonious community relations and to co-ordinate on a national basis the measures adopted for that purpose by others; and

(b) to advise the Secretary of State for the Home Department on any matter referred to the Commission by him and to make recommendations to him, on any matter which the Commission considers should be brought to his attention.

The Commission has published a variety of studies on aspects of community relations and its Education Department produces material appropriate for use by lecturers and students.

4 Centre for Information on Language Teaching (CILT),
  State House,
  63 High Holborn,
  London WC1.

CILT was established in 1966 to collect and co-ordinate information about all aspects, especially the teaching, of modern languages. This information is available to individuals and organizations professionally concerned with language teaching. CILT can provide advice to teachers and teacher-trainers and has up-to-date information about teaching methods and materials.

CILT, together with the English Teaching Information Centre of the British Council (ETIC) maintains a Language Teaching Library and an Audio-Visual Library which can be used for reference and research. The latter includes facilities for listening to recorded material and for viewing slides and film-strips. The CILT 'Register of Current Research' covers all disciplines relating to language teaching, and the Centre also produces 'Select Lists' (short introductory bibliographies for language teachers, including some relating to English for immigrants), 'Lists of Teaching Materials', 'Information Guides' and 'Information Papers', A leaflet giving details of these services is available on request.

5 Friends Community Relations Committee,
  Friends House,
  Euston Road,
  London NW1 2BJ.

The Friends Community Relations Committee is one of the component committees of the Social Responsibility Council of the Religious Society of Friends. The Committee concentrates on the race relations situation in Britain, and is involved in on-going activities and research work at national and local level. Further information and resource material available on application.

6 Institute of Race Relations,
  74 Shakespeare Road,
  London SE24 0PP.

The Institute of Race Relations is an unofficial and non-political body, founded in 1958, to encourage and facilitate the study of the relations between races everywhere. It has published a wide variety of studies on aspects of community relations. The institute has an extensive library of international literature, chiefly concerned with the Third World.

7 Local Community Relations Officers.

There are over eighty local Community Relations Officers working throughout the country in areas where minority groups are concentrated. Many Community Relations Officers are able to offer advice to colleges on setting up multicultural studies courses, particularly on arranging relevant fieldwork experience for students. A full list of Community Relations Councils is available from the Community Relations Commissions, 15/16 Bedford Street, London WC2.

8 The Media Resources Centre of the Inner London Education
    Authority,
   Highbury Station Road,
   Islington,
   London NI ISB.

The Media Resources Centre produces both materials (for example, packs on Black Studies, Indian history) and lists of resource information. Details of published material and on-going work can be obtained on application.

9 National Association for Multiracial Education (NAME),
   19 Margreave Road,
   Chaddesden,
   Derby,
   DE2 6JD.

NAME was formerly the National Federation of Association for the Education of Pupils from Overseas (ATEPO). The new association has wider aims than that which it replaces. The local NAME associations are concerned to help teachers in multiracial areas. They are particularly interested in the problems of language teaching, both to non-English speakers and over the whole school curriculum, and to relevant areas outside it. Teaching English is seen as a means rather than as an end in itself. Conference, workshop, discussions, study groups and exhibitions are organized, in many cases with the assistance of Local Education Authorities and teachers' centres.

10 National Book League,
   7 Albermarle Street,
   London WIX 4BB.

The National Book League has touring exhibitions on 'Books for the Multi-racial Classroom' and on English Language work with 'immigrant' children. The first contains books on India, Pakistan and the West Indies, etc. A printed, annotated book-list is available with the exhibition. The exhibition focussing on Language work contains 460 items, includes books on the teaching of English as a second language, immigrant background, stimuli to correct pronunciation and information, dictionaries and visual aids. A fully annotated booklist accompanies the exhibition.

11 Race Relations Board, (RRB),
   5 Lower Belgrave Street,
   London SWIW ONR.

The Race Relations Board is a statutory body set up to secure compliance with the Race Relations Act of 1968. It does this in the first instance by conciliation committees. Only where conciliation fails are remedies sought in the courts. The board will willingly give advice on matters falling within its jursidiction, and answer enquiries.

12 Royal Anthropological Society,
   36 Craven Street,
   London WC2N 5NG.

The Royal Anthropological Society have compiled a folder giving a guide to resource materials. The folder is issued on a three yearly basis and will be kept up-to-date each three year period. This folder attempts to aid teachers locate resources available at present. The contents include lists of films with a brief description and cost, university departments where there is an interest in anthropology, and non-university teachers of anthropology, an extensive bibliography and miscellaneous information.

13 The Runnymede Trust,
Stuart House,
1 Tudor Street,
London EC4Y OAD.

The Runnymede Trust is an independent foundation set up to provide information and to promote public education in race relations. The Trust has published a wide variety of studies on aspects of community relations; a full list of these can be obtained on application.

14 School of Oriental and African Studies,
Malet Street,
London, WC1.

The Extramural Studies Division of London University's School of Oriental and African Studies offers help to teachers and colleges of education with courses on Africa and Asia. This help takes three forms. First the Division can provide lecturers from the school's staff to give lectures or seminars in courses on geography, history, art, music, literature, religion and general studies. Secondly, the School can organize conferences on specific geographical areas or on themes, such as Development, to support programmes of work being done in schools and colleges. Thirdly, the Division runs a Resource Centre at 2–3 Bloomsbury Square, London WC1, which contains a selection of reference books, a selection of books for use by secondary school pupils and a collection of printed and duplicated material produced by a range of organizations, charities, governments, pressure groups. All material in the Resource Centre is card indexed by area for easy reference. There is a small collection of audio-visual material and also a card-index, by area, to all audio-visual material available in the United Kingdom on Asia and Africa. The Centre is open from 10.00 a.m. to 5.00 p.m. all week days and teachers are welcome to use the facilities available for examining books and material on Asia and Africa. There is however at present no loan system.

15 Voluntary Committee on Overseas Aid and Development (VCOAD),
   Parnell House,
   25 Wilton Road,
   London SWIV IJS.

The Education Unit of VCOAD co-ordinates the educational work in Britain of various overseas aid charities, such as Oxfam, Christian Aid and War on Want. VCOAD provides teaching materials for pupils, student teachers and teachers doing work on developing countries. Full details of resources available on request.

Index